The Children Can't Wait

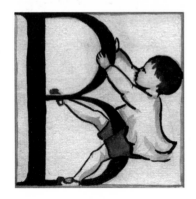

Deptford Forum Publishing Ltd
441 New Cross Road
London SE14 6TA
Published as a contribution to the
work of the McMillan Legacy Group

First published December 1999
© McMillan Legacy Group

Written by
Hayley Trueman
Emily Adlington
Frances Marriott
Deptford Discovery Team

Edited by
Jess Steele

Design & typesetting by
Lionel Openshaw

**Printed and bound
in Great Britain by**
Biddles Ltd, Guildford

Photographs from
Lewisham Local Studies Centre
Lewisham Library
199-201 Lewisham High Street
London SE13
and
Rachel McMillan Nursery School
Deptford Green, London SE8

Illustrations from
The Mary Peet Archive

Typeset in
Filosofia 10/12
& Base-Nine 8.3/12
[Emigre® Fonts]

**British Library Cataloguing
in Publication Data**

A catalogue record for this book is
available from the British Library

ISBN 1 898536 81 3

CONTENTS

ACKNOWLEDGMENTS

Lionel Openshaw for design, advice and editorial assistance, Nadine Gahr for helping-out with design and production, and Trisha Lee for rescue co-ordination at a crisis moment

Barbara Furneaux (who gave us the Mary Peet archive), Mary Clarke, Mary Puddephat, Sue Pittman, and all former staff, students and pupils who were so generous with their memories

Groundwork *Vital Centres & Green Links* SRB and the Creekside Renewal Programme for funding assistance to the McMillan Legacy Group since January 1997

Deborah & David Head at the Ashburnham Arms for their hospitality and excellent refreshments

Alison Gough, former archivist responsible for the McMillan archive at the University of Greenwich

This book is dedicated to
Margaret & Rachel McMillan and to all the members of the McMillan Legacy Group

Many thanks to
The McMillan Legacy Group committee members who have each played their own special role in creating this book and furthering the vision of a McMillan 'eco-system of early years'.

Emily Adlington
Nicola Amies
Jayne Day
Iris Dove
Frances Marriott
Julia Philipps
Portia Smith
Jess Steele
Roger Sedgely
Wendy Titman
Hayley Trueman
Suzanne Tyler
Andrew Winter

INTRODUCTION
by Jess Steele

Margaret and Rachel McMillan swept away old ideas to create a revolution in the care, health and education of young children. Their vision and perseverance changed the way children were treated on every level, from the most practical nurture to a new educational curriculum.

Each stage of development in the McMillan 'eco-system' of early years led directly from the lessons they were learning. Their tireless crusade to break the vicious circle of bad nourishment, poor conditions and disease led to the clinics and school medical treatment. The repetition of illness among poorer children despite treatment led to the innovation of the night camps and the focus on bathing, healthy food and fresh air. Slowly the camps became established as the Nursery School and the educational content increased. As more and more students came to work and study at the nursery it was necessary to build a separate Training College building. Margaret's last dream – to give children a taste of the country beyond Deptford's horizon – came true soon after her death when the holiday home was built at Wrotham in Kent.

Margaret McMillan – prolific in her writings, an energetic and inspiring speaker, a community activist with vision and great practical ability – must rank as one of the hardest workers this country has ever seen. After the devastation of Rachel's death in 1917, Margaret's determination to nurture and educate "each child as if he were your own" became further entrenched. Her socialist politics remained at the core of her approach but, as she was so keenly aware, the children can't wait for revolution.

Margaret was instrumental in the earliest medical inspections of school children, the first school meals (and baths), the use of fresh air and exercise, play and affection as basic tools in childcare and child development.

I loved Miss McMillan very dearly, and owe a great deal to her. She was a tall, well-built woman with a mop of unruly hair, which I often pinned up for her. She always wore a long gold chain which she fingered frequently, especially when she was cross with us.
Rosie Cawte (Pupil 1914 - 26)

Margaret McMillan was a fighter. Her enemies were ignorance, prejudice, dirt and disease. She said "to be weak is to be wicked; to stand still is to go back". Her last message to her students was: "Tell my girls to stick to the slums. Many teachers can be found for schools set in pleasant places. The bravest and best are needed for the slums."
Emma Stevinson, *Rachel McMillan Training College Newsletter***, July 1931**

[5]

She was not only one of the best women of her time... but also one of the most cantankerous, and she owed a great deal of her effectiveness to the latter useful quality.
George Bernard Shaw

Her reputation brought students from all over the world to work with her in Deptford. Insisting on the need for proper training for nursery teachers, she also expected them to understand the living conditions of the children they were to serve. McMillan was well known for persistence at the Board of Education, waiting all day on the Ministry steps if necessary.

The vicious circle of poor environment–poor health–poor achievement is still very much with us. The lives and work of Margaret and Rachel McMillan are as relevant now as at any time in the last hundred years. There can be no doubt about the level of interest, nationally and locally, in the issues around early years care and education. Both sides of the 'childcare' equation are under intense debate: on one hand the Government's desire to get single mothers into work relies on high-quality, widely-available, affordable childcare; on the other its commitment to standards in education and challenging youth

crime depends on a sound base for children's social and learning development. The Labour Party committed itself in January 1997 to establishing an "integrated and coherent early years service" bringing together education, care and family support for all young children. It recognised the inadequacy of current training for work with young children and has since developed the National Childcare Strategy to address these issues.

Despite a very welcome understanding of the importance of childcare and early years education, the struggle continues between those who embrace the McMillan philosophy of 'learning through play' and those who would return to an approach more like the old Board Schools where lines of toddlers sat quiet, hands behind their backs and learned by rote.

This is a source-book for the McMillan story, tales for the classroom and the pub, a conference or a sunny afternoon in the Rachel Mac nursery gardens.

THE McMILLANS 1860 - 1931
by Hayley Trueman

On 29 March 1931, Margaret McMillan died in a Harrow nursing home at the age of seventy. The last 27 years of her life had been spent working in Deptford. It was there, with the help of her sister, Rachel, that she established a health treatment clinic for local school children, night camps, and finally the Rachel McMillan Nursery School and Training Centre.

It is for this work that she is best remembered, yet it was the culmination of a lifetime spent working for social welfare and justice. Margaret McMillan was a committed Christian socialist; a prolific journalist and writer who penned hundreds of articles, stories and books during her life; and a shrewd political activist who took up many causes from dockers' pay to women's suffrage. She was an important figure of many political organisations, including the Independent Labour Party and the Nursery Association, at both local and national levels.

Though from a Scottish highlands family, both Margaret and Rachel McMillan were born in Westchester, New York State: Rachel in 1859, followed closely by Margaret in 1860, and in 1862 a third sister, Elizabeth, who was to die at the age of three. Their father, James McMillan, had emigrated to America with his new wife Jean Cameron in 1858. Following the death of her husband and daughter in the summer of 1865, Jean Cameron decided to return with Margaret and Rachel to her parents in Scotland.

Keen that her daughters would receive an education, their mother sent both to the Inverness High School. Rachel was later sent to a boarding school for 'young ladies' in Coventry and Margaret to the Inverness Academy. Margaret McMillan later claimed that her time at school, "where the girls were such dreadful snobs" had made a rebel and reformer out of her.

Rachel & Margaret as young girls

McMillan in Geneva, c. 1880

Their mother and grandfather both died in 1877, leaving Rachel the burden of caring for their elderly and infirm grandmother. However, for Margaret the years following her mother's death were full of interest and wonder. She was sent to study music at Frankfurt and languages at Geneva and Lausanne, with a view to preparing her for work as a governess.

When the sisters' grandmother died in July 1888, Rachel looked for paid employment. She moved to London, taking the job of Junior Superintendent in a young women's hostel in Bloomsbury. Not long after, Margaret gave up her work as a governess and joined her sister. Together they began to attend socialist meetings and made personal contact with people many regarded as agitators. They were introduced to William Morris, and to H M Hyndham of the Social Democratic Foundation. They became involved with the Fabian Society and met with Bernard Shaw, Annie Besant, and Sydney and Beatrice Webb. They knew

anarchists, too, such as Prince Kropotkin and Louise Michel.

Step by step the McMillans moved from being spectators to workers for the socialist movement. They began to address meetings at dock and factory gates on Sunday mornings, selling political papers such as *Justice* and *Commonweal*. Margaret also took up voluntary work in Whitechapel, holding singing classes for jam and mill girls who often jeered at her, calling her a toff.

The small amounts of money Margaret made writing articles for newspapers was not enough to make a living, so she decided to seek work as a governess again. She obtained several interviews but once she explained that she was a socialist her interviewers lost interest in her. Finally she was offered an interview for the position of governess to an adopted child of Lady Meux of Park Lane, wife of Sir Henry Meux the wealthy brewer and baronet. At the interview, in her customary fashion, Margaret McMillan declared herself to be a socialist, asking Lady Meux if she was one too. " I, a socialist?" replied Lady Meux with some amusement. "Look at my rings" she said, showing Margaret her hands which were adorned with diamond encrusted rings. Undeterred by Margaret's political leanings, Lady Meux offered her a job as her personal companion: the job of governess was never, in fact, real. Margaret accepted but once she had taken up her position Lady Meux began to dictate that she should abandon socialism. Lady Meux also decided that Margaret should be trained as an actress, receiving tuition in breathing, singing and voice.

Margaret McMillan now led a curious dual existence, on the one hand continuing to involve herself in socialist political activity and, on the other, training for the stage under the patronage of a titled woman. The conflict between her political beliefs and her job came to a head on May Day 1892, when Margaret made a speech on a socialist platform in Hyde Park,

in support of the striking dockers. Lady Meux was furious when she found out and accused Margaret of "going about with dreadful people". Margaret was presented with an ultimatum: to reject socialism and continue in her job or leave immediately. She decided to turn her back on comfort and security for the challenges that socialist activity held.

Thus, in 1893 she and Rachel left London for Bradford where they joined the newly formed Independent Labour Party (ILP). Margaret began to lecture, write and organise unpaid on a full-time basis, relying on Rachel to keep them both. In the following year she took up one of the rare opportunities for service in the public sector open to women when she was elected to the Bradford School Board. Greatly disturbed by what she observed – neglected children at every stage of illness, suffering from rickets, curvature of the spine, adenoids and dirt-borne diseases – she embarked upon the indomitable task of improving the

Lady Meux... had been a pantomime girl at the Surrey Music Hall and a barmaid at the Horseshoe Tavern, next door to the Meux's brewery in Tottenham Court Road... It was written of her that: "Hers is one of the most picturesque of the rags-to-riches or whore-house to manor-house sagas." She came to be on intimate terms with Sir Henry at the Casino de Venise in Holborn... [His] liaison with her was a social scandal. The stigma attached to her kind of lifestyle was hard to remove.
Elizabeth Bradburn,
Margaret McMillan – Portrait of a Pioneer

McMillan in Bradford, c. 1901

condition of school children. From the washing of diseased and filthy children, ("how can you educate a dirty child?" she asked passionately), to the writing of pamphlets to advise parents on hygiene, she moved onwards to campaign for school medical inspections, school clinics, and school meals.

Within a few years she had been successful in establishing official school baths, unofficial school medical inspections, school meals for poor children (by voluntary effort) and had helped parents and teachers come to a better understanding of the need to improve the health and well-being of young children.

In 1902 the Conservative Government's Education Act abolished School Boards and placed their duties in the hands of urban district and county councils – to which women could not be elected. The result of this was that Margaret McMillan and all the other women on the School Boards were forced to resign. Ill with exhaustion and deprived of an important

activity, Margaret left Bradford in November 1902 and headed back to London, where her fight to improve the lives of poor children was to take her back to some of the poorest areas of London.

Joining Rachel (who was now employed by Kent County Council as a teacher of hygiene) in 51 Tweedy Road, Bromley, Margaret McMillan took up a lectureship with the London Ethical Society, part of the humanist and rationalist movement in Britain. She was employed as a paid full-time worker, promoting ideas on educational issues through public lectures. This work would continue until the First World War, giving her the opportunity to develop and express her philosophies on childhood and education to a wide audience. By 1904 she had also joined the newly formed Workers' Educational Association, and become an executive member of the Froebel Society. Her journalism also increasingly covered the subjects of education and child welfare. Margaret McMillan's interest in educational and societal reform extended to the friendships she developed with distinguished reformers and educationalists such as Stanton Coit, Kropotkin, the Cobden-Sandersons and Albert Mansbridge, all of whom were regular visitors to the house in Bromley.

How many lions she bearded in their dens I do not know. Prime ministers of State, MPs, Councillors, writers and important citizens — she was daunted by none of them and, when overwhelmed by fatigue, illness or depression she would continue to plead her cause to anyone with power or influence, including Royalty.
Margaret Lamming (Student 1923 - 25)

Margaret McMillan was an orator and also very much a seer. Her early adhesion to the Socialist movement was the means by which Labour was to become the greatest force for education of all the parties. She was in fact the architect of Labour's education ideas.
William Leach, 'In Memory of Margaret McMillan' *The Labour Woman*, May 1931

Often at election times one is tempted to wonder if people realise what is behind 'social questions'? The meetings this year were attended mostly by men. There was hardly a woman present at any gathering I witnessed; and the men were interested very greatly in trams (which was natural) and also in cinematographs (which is childish). They showed no interest in the question of medical treatment and as for education, it meant for them a process that is concerned mainly with desks and superannuation grants.
Margaret McMillan, *The Christian World*, 27 March 1913

[Margaret McMillan] brought with her a sense of largeness. One had a feeling that she breathed a larger atmosphere, and lived and moved among larger things than ordinary men and women.
P B Ballard, *Margaret McMillan: An Appreciation*

*In 1922 my mother took me from afflu-
ent Sidcup… down to the slums of
Deptford to meet Margaret McMillan.
Crowded, dirty and depressing streets —
the houses, shops and pubs squalid
and derelict. Babies and small children
playing on roads and pavements, and
sprawling on doorsteps. Many underground rooms in damp basements with
metal grills on which one stepped,
seemingly on the heads of the families
living in the underground accommodation. Children, often sewn into their
clothes, with running sores, streaming
noses and limbs bent with rickets were
all too evident … I wondered where on
earth my mother was taking me.*
**Margaret Lamming
(Student 1923 - 25)**

*My mother and grandparents… were so
horrified by the general drabness and
poverty… driving down Church Street,
that my grandfather said, "we can't
leave the child here".*
**Winifred Brown
(Student 1928 – 31)**

The McMillans in Deptford

In her book *The Life of Rachel
McMillan* Margaret McMillan wrote
that it was during this stay in Bromley
that Rachel took a walk to the Greenwich observatory, eventually wander-
ing over the border into Deptford.
Margaret dramatically describes Deptford as:"the place of the deep ford.
Very deep and steep it is, the soft black
yielding mass under the black waters
of poverty. At every step one goes
down and down."

She described the terrible scenes
Rachel observed: "stained and tumb-
ling walls, the dark, noisy courts, the
crowded rooms, the sodden alleys all
hidden behind roaring streets. Women
who care no more. Girls whose youth is
a kind of defiance. Children creeping
on the filthy pavement, half naked, un-
washed and covered with sores."

Margaret first encountered Deptford and its children at close hand in
1904, when she was appointed Manager for Alverton Street, Trundley's
Road and Deptford Park Schools.

Deptford was one of the most
built-up areas of London and one of
the poorest. In 1911 the population for
the Borough of Deptford numbered
109,000. There was a density of 72
persons per acre in Deptford, compared to Lewisham with 25 and Greenwich with 26 per acre. In the East
Ward where the McMillans would do
much of their work, the density was
131 people per acre.

Most families lived in one-roomed
tenements that served as living room,
kitchen and bedroom. With barely enough room for two beds, families often
slept in one bed at the end of the
room. With the average number of
children in a family being five, over-
crowding was a terrible problem.
Most, if not all, of the children in the
McMillans' catchment area came from
over-crowded homes. Even as late as
1930, around 30% of the McMillans'
pupils lived in one-roomed apart-
ments in sub-divided houses. There
was a shortage of good, reasonably-
priced housing available to poor

working families, and what was available was in a terrible condition. Although at this time there was legislation to ensure that homes should be properly repaired, free from damp, well-ventilated and have adequate sanitation, enforcement was proving impossible.

Most men in the East Ward were unskilled labourers finding casual work in the docks, engineering, brick, tin, sack and jam manufacturing works. The women could find employment as seamstresses, domestic servants or in some factories. The average wage for 83% of the population was twenty shillings. Many earned far less than this, but even twenty shillings was nowhere near enough to meet the barest physical needs of any family in East Deptford. As the causes of infant mortality were poverty, malnutrition, over-crowding and lack of sleep, it is easy to see why it was so high in Deptford, with approximately one fifth of all children born in the East Ward failing to make it through life's first year.

As a manager of a group of Deptford schools, McMillan's attention increasingly focused on the education and developmental health of young children and their relationship to home life. The plight of the youngest children became even more embedded in her developing philosophy when, in 1905, Article 53 of the Education Code stated that under-fives should be removed from the infants departments of elementary schools. This caused a dramatic drop in the number of three to five year olds in schools. The dozens of toddlers that the McMillans encountered playing in the gutters of Deptford after 1905 were a direct result of this Education Code directive. The sudden lack of educational provision for under-fives is likely to have influenced Margaret McMillan to move towards the development of the 'Baby Camp' and later the 'Nursery School'.

Meanwhile, she was preoccupied by the need for medical inspections and treatments in schools. The

The staple trade of the district [of Deptford] is a horrible one. It is cattle slaughtering. The men butcher of course, but the girls and women clean entrails… in some streets there is always an odour of death. In many streets there are public houses and on holidays the street opposite the bar door is packed with perambulators. On summer days you see scores of dirty, uncombed and ragged children playing on the hot pavements. Pretty baby hands seize refuse from the gutter. A bundle of dirty rags on a doorstep turns over and lo! A charming baby face.
Margaret McMillan,
'A Flower in the Slum'
The Christian Commonwealth
14 September 1910

[Margaret McMillan] works for the children of the very poor, and she has succeeded in putting some very important things through for their benefit. She told me how very serious the conditions are under which the great majority of the English people now live. They are so bad in fact that the average child of the workman is threatened with lifelong invalidism. Miss McMillan has established some night camps where sick children can sleep in the fresh air, receive proper medical treatment and physical training and thus gain a better chance to escape the horrible influences of the slum...

Helen Keller,
Letter to her mother Kate, 1912

Sanatoria, housing, pensions, scholarships, even better wages – what are these without early culture or education? Sour apples grown on hungry land. The first years decide all."

Margaret McMillan,
Nursery Schools and the
***Pre-school Child*, 1918**

diseased and filthy children she encountered during her first two years as a Deptford schools manager led her to question (as she had in Bradford) how children could possibly benefit from education when their health was continuously poor? Unless the situation was quickly corrected, the children who suffered from the disease of poverty would grow into adults whose own children, in turn, would experience the same desperate childhoods. The cycle of inequality and poverty would thus continue generation after generation. The children she met in the schools and on the streets of Deptford had already to a certain degree been destroyed by the poverty bound up in their lives. Margaret McMillan yearned to change the system which created these abhorrent conditions. Yet she was realistic enough to see that sick children could not wait for political reform: "How cheery and high-hearted [Fred] is", she observed in her article 'Camp Schools', "yet at the same time one can see that hunger and

the misery at home are bearing a little too hard on Fred. What do I propose? Reform the land laws? Bring in socialism? Destroy capitalism? Yes! But in the meanwhile? You see, Fred is twelve. In four years from now it will be too late to help him."

Her plan of action was set: to work with the children, and to keep up the fight for political change as well.

The Clinics

In November 1904 Margaret McMillan approached the London County Council (LCC) with plans for a scheme to provide and equip a number of health centres across London for the treatment of school children. Backed with an offer of £5,000 from Joseph Fels, an American philanthropist and millionaire soap manufacturer, she sent the scheme to Sir Robert Morant, Permanent Secretary to the Government's Board of Education, whom she had met in Bradford when campaigning for school baths. He willingly placed it before the Education Committee, but the application was refused. A year later another scheme for the provision of health centres was presented to the committee by Margaret McMillan and her colleagues, as managers of a group of schools in Deptford. The scheme was again turned down on the grounds that the LCC had no public duty in law to provide medical and welfare attention for school children. This must have seemed a poor excuse to Margaret McMillan who knew that a few local authorities, like Bradford, had already managed to provide school medical inspections and feed needy school children under existing legislation.

In 1905 Margaret McMillan campaigned to persuade Parliament to back a Bill that contained a clause to establish compulsory medical inspection of school children. She wished to establish the principle that child health and welfare were an essential part of the education system rather than just an aspect of public health, and predicted that compulsory school medical inspection would be the stepping stone towards establishing school treatment centres. She knew the time was right to lobby for legislative change. The Government's alarm at the recent disclosures of a report examining the levels of poverty and ill health among the working classes, especially children, signalled a shift in the political climate around social welfare and health.

We all hate the poverty – and the riches – of capitalist society. But the real poverty goes deeper than wages. It is in the starved, cramped, diseased bodies and minds; the eyes that do not see; the ears that do not hear; how can we change them?
Margaret McMillan

[Margaret McMillan] hoped the [clinic] would be a beacon of light in Deptford. She remembered some of the greatest admirals were born in Deptford. In Deptford some of England's most illustrious men were born and lived. There in Deptford the great English fleet was founded, and she believed there was great material in the streets of Deptford. Although the streets were disfigured by poverty there was something in the hearts of the people which would in time rise superior to the surroundings.
'The Opening of the Deptford Clinic', *South Eastern Herald* **22 July 1910**

Back into Watergate Street. South of Prince Street character rapidly deteriorates… all is poor. Old houses, mostly three-storey, let in tenements. Faint foetid smell prevails, overpowered in places by disgusting stench. Rough women, one with head bandaged, others with black eyes. One old harridan sitting on doorstep with a dirty clay pipe, shoeless children.
George Arkell, one of Charles Booth's researchers, Walk 38, 26 July 1899, *The Streets of London: The Booth Notebooks*

The Inter-Departmental Committee on Physical Deterioration which compiled the report in 1904, had been set up as a response to the startling revelations made in several pioneering sociological reports, including Charles Booth's *Life and Labour of the People of London* (1891) and Seebohm Rowntree's *Poverty: A Study of Town Life* (1901). The 1904 report challenged 19th century assumptions that poverty among the working classes was the result of weakness of character and unwillingness to work. It also demonstrated that charity and poor relief were ineffective in eradicating the problems of poverty. It went on to recommend that "a systemised medical inspection of children at school should be imposed on every school authority as a public duty" and also that local authorities should be given the responsibility for feeding needy school children.

The eventual passing of the Education (Administrative Provisions) Act of 1907 allowed the Board of Education to set up a medical department and implement medical inspections. It also gave some limited powers to local authorities to provide medical treatment for school children. This Act also paved the way for the establishment of school clinics. In July 1908 the Government gave permission, under certain conditions, for the opening of school clinics and in December that year McMillan opened the first of her experimental school treatment centres in Bow. At that time there were only three clinics recorded in Britain; by 1930 there were no less than 1,741 throughout the country.

The Bow Clinic functioned from a small upper room belonging to the headmistress of the Devons Road School, serving the children of that one school. The LCC rented the room to the clinic and offered no financial help in its running nor took any interest in its progress. Joseph Fels met most of the costs, and the clinic was managed by the Metropolitan District ILP Committee for the Physical

Welfare of Children. In her article 'A Plea for School Clinics' (1909), Margaret McMillan described those who came to the Bow Clinic for treatment: "A few of the children are rickety ... [most] are too light and are plainly under-nourished. One girl staggered as she left the clinic, and it was found that she had had no food for a long time. A great many suffer from another starvation: they never have enough sleep."

Despite these ailments McMillan optimistically described how:"with a month of regular ear-syringing, a few meals or a food tonic from the doctor's shelf, a little care under direction, and hey-presto! the small sufferer lifts like a flower in the sun."

Even though nearly 80 of the 141 children treated in the first six months were cured of their ills, the clinic remained vulnerable. Without LCC financial backing, and because the Bow Clinic served only one school, it was not financially viable. Treatment cost seven shillings and sixpence per child compared with five shillings that hospitals charged. The clinic would have to close.

When Margaret McMillan was offered the use of St Nicholas' vestry in Deptford, rent free by Greenwich Borough Council, she gladly accepted and proceeded to move the treatment centre from Bow to Deptford. The new clinic would operate as the treatment centre to the group of Deptford schools where she was manager. The move took place in June 1910, and the clinic was formally opened on 15 July.

The Vestry House was situated in Deptford Green opposite St Nicholas' Churchyard. There was a small downstairs waiting room and a first floor medical treatment room, including a dentist's chair and a dark room for eye examinations. Two doctors, a dentist, a full-time nurse, a remedial drill teacher and a caretaker were employed by the clinic. Money was tight as the clinic still received no financial help from the local authority. It was funded by private charity and through fees

Dentist at work in the Deptford clinic, 1911

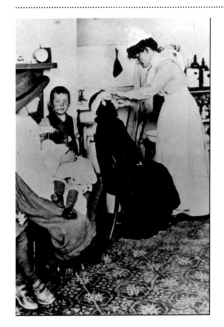

The Nurse inspecting eyes and ears at the Deptford clinic

By the end of the Summer, 29 children were living and sleeping in the camp. There was hardly any illness even during the hot months... there seems to have been marked mental improvement as well as physical... It has been generally recognised that the proper care of children under school age forms a serious gap in the measures that have been suggested to ensure a healthier and more vigorous people. This open-air camp for these babies is an endeavour to bridge the gap, and it is a method of treatment and child nurture that might well be encouraged and developed.
Dr Eder, Senior Medical Officer at the Deptford Clinic, August 1914

Nurse comes every day at four, and the children troop in to have eyes bathed, ears syringed... They are so fond of her. She has soft hands, and she is not tall – just big enough to put a kind arm on your shoulders if you are in trouble.
Margaret McMillan
'The Deptford Clinic'
The Clarion, 29 July 1910

paid by the parents. Despite the financial problems McMillan and her staff managed to turn the clinic into a successful venture. The cost of treatment with full attendance, fell to two shillings and nine pence per child.

Even so, McMillan was only too aware of the constraints that had been placed upon the Bow Clinic by the lack of local authority financial backing. Thus, after six months she produced a report on the clinic's work which convinced the LCC to give McMillan her first grant in March 1911: two shillings for each dental case treated and £300 towards the dentist's salary. Over the next three years the grant was extended to the treatment of ear and eye cases and by 1915 all the work of the clinic was financed by the LCC.

The clinic grew and flourished. In 1911 John Evelyn, the local MP, and his wife approached Margaret McMillan with the offer of a property at 353 Evelyn Street (later known as Evelyn House), rent free for use in the course of her work. McMillan accepted, and the sisters moved into the house to organise the new clinic extension. A small operating theatre was set up for the treatment of tonsil and adenoid cases and the old drawing room was turned into a ward. Operations took place on Saturdays and patients would be cared for by the McMillan sisters while they recovered. For five days of the week the operating room was adapted and used for remedial drill work, where children were taught special exercises designed to improve breathing and correct spine defects.

Even though the clinic was proving to be successful, Margaret McMillan became increasingly dissatisfied. The patients were drawn from a wide area and consisted of both middle and working class children. She had observed that, while middle class children benefited greatly from the treatment they received from the clinic, the poorer children made little or no progress. In her book *The Camp School* (1917) she describes how the poor children came to the clinic at all hours

Category	Boys	Girls	Infants
Medically Examined	383	408	342
Cases of Defect	192	209	117
Received Treatment	92	51	22
Cured	60	30	7
Receiving Free Meals	115	92	64
Defective Teeth	87%	86%	51%
Eye Defects	73	102	16
Ear Defects	19	37	47
Nose Defects	10	4	10
Adenoids	28	16	4
Tonsils	43	45	36
Anæmic	28	13	—
Sundry Defects	5	4	4

'New School Clinic at Deptford – Figures for Children at Creek Road School'
***Christian Commonwealth*, July 1910**

Children were taught special exercises designed to improve breathing and correct spine defects

and always in large numbers: "they poured into the waiting room, they streamed into the treatment room at all hours of the day, and nearly always the case was so urgent that to delay treatment was cruel... it was relief work in many cases – a kind of First Aid."

She increasingly saw the clinic as giving only temporary relief to the children. "'Here is the School Clinic at last' it may be said. 'This will end all the misery!' What! End it – a clinic? The roots of all this misery are so deep and strong... "

The real suffering had to be addressed at its roots. She noted that time and money was wasted on just repairing the damage: "Let me give you one example", she wrote, "in the three last months... our nurse treated 950 cases of skin disease. Within the same period 927 of these returned, after being cured, to have the same kind of disease treated by drug and lotion. Hundreds came back five and even six times within twelve months. Of what use is all this labour and expense? Who benefits by it?"

Margaret McMillan was desperate to find the solution to these problems. In March 1911, she and Rachel started to clear and level the garden of Evelyn House. After white-washing the walls and constructing shelters and beds from gas piping, trestles and canvas, the first open air night camp was ready to welcome the children.

[20]

The Girls' Night Camp

Girls who had been attending the clinic began to stay overnight in the garden of Evelyn House, as an experiment devised by Margaret McMillan, to prove that fresh air, exercise and good nutritious food would improve their health in a way that the clinic could not. The first camper was a girl of seven called Marigold. Anæmic and on the verge of consumption, she was living in the noisy back streets of Deptford with her father who was a hawker. Her clothing was poor and her boots full of holes.

The remedial teacher Miss Ridell became the camp headmistress, supervising girls ranging in age from six to fourteen. As many as seventeen girls would sleep there watched over by a woman camp guardian, who was given a lantern and hand bell with which she could summon the caretaker in an emergency.

The camp routine was kept simple. The girls would arrive early evening and were given tasks to complete. At

Girls preparing for bed in the Girls' Night Camp

The boiler was also used for making porridge, dumplings and steamed pudding at breakfast and supper

6.30 pm 'washing rites' began. The older girls took charge of the younger ones, seeing to hair, nails, teeth and bathing. The camp beds would then be put up and made up with sheets, pillows and warm blankets that had been dyed blue especially for the camp. The beds were positioned facing south east to catch the early morning sunlight. The little ones were asleep by 7.45 pm and the rest of the girls would be in bed by 8 pm, reassured by the gentle glow of the red lantern.

The children had breakfast at the camp – porridge bought from Inverness: "once we got lowland meal and once English meal, and on both occasions the girls' weight went down at a run in a week!" recalled Margaret.

The girls left for the local elementary school at a quarter to nine, and ate their two other meals at home. The simple principle behind all of this was to get the girls out of the cramped and badly ventilated bedrooms and give them a good night's sleep.

Margaret McMillan initially saw the development of the Night Camp as an essential extension of the school clinic, announcing that the clinic was the nursery of the poor, adapted to the exigencies of working class life. Her intention was not to remove children from their homes and neighbourhood, but to provide an extension to them, "an open-air residential school, that does not separate the child from his home".

The Boys' Camp

Encouraged by the success of the Girls' Night Camp, Margaret McMillan hoped to extend the experiment and began looking for a site upon which to open a camp for the local boys.

The vicar of St Nicholas' Church gave permission for the McMillans to make use of the churchyard. Early in 1912 they set up a temporary shelter near to the grave of Admiral Benbow. Unfortunately they were ordered to remove it within a few days by the council surveyor, so the Old Vestry Hall was used as the night shelter during bad weather.

Initially eight Deptford boys were allowed by their parents to attend the night camp. This rose to between a dozen and sixteen boys sleeping out every night in the churchyard on beds made from gas pipes, trestles and French flour sacks. An old boiler supplied hot water for the tin baths where the boys washed before going to bed. The boiler was also used for making porridge, dumplings and steamed pudding at breakfast and supper.

During the day the boys received schooling in the churchyard, sitting out on church pews under the trees, and were encouraged to help with the tending of vegetable plots that Margaret McMillan had established down one side of the churchyard. After a month of outdoor living the boys' health began to improve, though little progress was made with schooling. In *The Camp School* Margaret McMillan described the impact of camp life upon the boys, "we had some good results; not as regards school teaching,

for I am bound to say the boys seemed determined to learn nothing of that kind. They merely began at once to get stronger and healthier."

The camp began to receive much publicity, both good and bad. It was featured in an article that appeared in the *Daily Mirror* on 11 June 1912. Photographs of small boys sleeping among the gravestones, and making porridge dominated the front page. The newspaper praised the camp as a "splendid scheme" and congratulated Margaret McMillan on her efforts to improve the lives of Deptford youngsters. The *Kentish Mercury* took a different view however, condemning Margaret McMillan for having secured the health of the boys by "growing broad beans and other esculents in the dust… of… Christopher Marlowe", who was buried there.

There was other criticism of the use of the churchyard. Visitors to the Camp talked of desecration and the dangers of noisy young boys disturbing the spirits of the dead. "Our hands

Of special interest was the open-air school and night camp close by. Boys who have been certified unfit to attend school… are received for a number of weeks… The specialty of this new work is that the children sleep in the night shelter. It is the open-air cure for them … Everything is done for the one important end – to establish the boys in health. A supper of milk and biscuits (rich in protein), or vegetables with dumplings is given. They breakfast on fine Highland oatmeal and milk.
'A School Health Centre: Pioneer Work at Deptford'
***Christian World*, 27 Feb 1913**

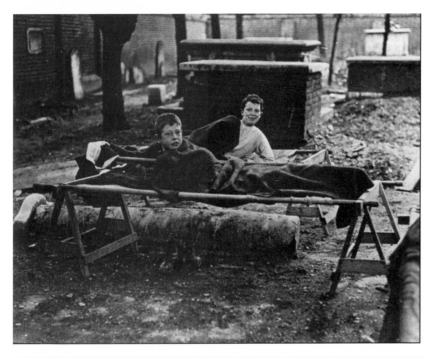

The boys slept among gravestones in the St Nicholas' churchyard camp

were tied", Margaret recalled in *The Camp School*, "our every movement watched, our life a burden. Besides the criticism, we had the wind and the rain and no cover." Giving way to local pressure, the McMillans began to look for another site and in April 1912 they found a piece of waste ground to rent in Hughes Fields, close to the clinic. It was on this site, which had been the dumping ground for twenty nearby houses and was approached by a narrow lane full of garbage, that the permanent camp school was eventually built.

Margaret McMillan designed and had built on the site a bath house which cost £30 and a shelter for £120. Within a month the boys had settled into the routine of the new camp. They had breakfast and supper at the camp, which they cooked themselves, but went back home for their dinners.

Baths were taken every night before bed. During the day the boys took lessons in the shed which doubled as a sleeping pavilion at night. The shed had a concrete floor and a permanently fixed back wall. The two side walls were simple partitions that could be removed or replaced in whole or part. The front of the shed was completely open but had a storm screen for use in bad weather. Along the back wall Margaret McMillan installed the camp library, with books full of adventure and travel. Pictures adorned the walls, and pots of plants and flowers covered every available surface. The seating doubled as storage lockers for the blankets and pillows. Each boy had his own locker with his name and number on it. The camp beds were stored in the opening between the back wall and the roof. The camp had a woodshed where wood-working was taught and a shed for the storage of the gardening tools.

The camp suffered from many teething problems in the first few months. It faced opposition from the local residents who took to hurling insults and rubbish at the camp, disturbing its activities.

In spite of all these frustrations, McMillan persevered. She employed three teachers to introduce the children to the subjects of history, geography, drama, arts and crafts and nature study. The boys took school drill and played both football and cricket. Margaret McMillan gave the older children lessons in English, dramatic art, literature, clear speech and movement.

By 1913 both the boys and the girls took lessons at the Boys' Camp, the girls returning to the garden of Evelyn House in the evening. By the outbreak of the First World War the camp catered for 17 girls and 40 boys.

The Baby Camp

Margaret McMillan was all too aware of the limited success she had achieved with the older children who attended the camp schools. Although the health and education of the children had improved during their time in the camps, many of the illnesses and problems they suffered from were

The boys broke the crockery… lost the towels… did all kinds of strange things with new toothbrushes. The thirst for knowledge may be great in the human of nine to twelve years old — if so, it had been quenched for the moment in most of our boys. Nevertheless… we began to draw, write and read a little. We wrote and drew very badly. Our spelling was inconceivable …once I showed them a page of Dickens. "He spells worse than us" they said gravely.
Margaret McMillan,
***The Camp School*, 1917**

[25]

The new Baby Camp at Hughes Fields recreation grounds

long-standing and recurring ones that had developed during early childhood. She believed that they were dealing with the children far too late – they needed help before the dirt and disease got a hold.

Now that the garden at Evelyn House was empty during the day, the decision was taken to open, for an experimental period, a small Nursery Camp. Rachel McMillan resigned from her Kent County Council job towards the end of 1913 so that she and her sister could give full attention to the work they were about to undertake. Six children under the age of five began to play and sleep in the garden of Evelyn House in early 1914, under the supervision of a Scottish teacher called Miss MacLeod. "This was the beginning of the Rachel McMillan Open-Air Nursery School and Training Centre", Margaret announced with ambition. The Nursery Camp was to be not only an open-air nursery school, but the seed from which other nursery schools would grow.

The Baby Camp, which eventually became the Rachel McMillan Open-Air Nursery School, was opened in April 1914 on a piece of land in Deptford Church Street. Joseph Fels, who was about to return to the United States, did one final service by writing to the LCC, suggesting that the McMillans be given the use of this vacant land, known as the Stowage, that lay in front of the Deptford Clinic. The LCC, which had originally wanted to build an elementary school on the site, agreed to rent the land and the use of a house to the McMillans for a shilling a year terminable at a day's notice, stipulating that no permanent structure was to be erected on the site.

Rachel was left to plan and organise the Baby Camp while Margaret recovered from injuries she received while attending a Women's Suffrage demonstration. As a member of the Committee for the Repeal of the Cat and Mouse Act (legislation that allowed the temporary release and then re-imprisonment of hunger strikers from gaol) she had attended the petitioning of the House of Commons, and had been violently thrown down the steps of Westminster by the police.

In March 1914, characteristically ignoring her agreement with the LCC not to build any permanent buildings, Margaret McMillan had the first of three shelters constructed and the small nursery from Evelyn House moved onto the site. By August this "wide and sunny place" was providing nurture for 29 children, from three months to five years old. Margaret McMillan recorded the ailments these new camp babies suffered on arrival: "tonsils, diseased glands, bad teeth, rickets, blepharitis, hernia, wasting, fits, rhinitis conjunctivitis, impetigo, cleft palate [and] bronchitis." On this acre of wasteland the McMillans began to develop the garden which became such an important part of their educational philosophy.

An organisation called the Vacant Lot Cultivation Group helped the McMillans to cultivate a show allot-

Our rickety children, our cramped and deformed children... get back to the earth with its magnetic currents, and free blowing wind... to let them live at last and have sight of people planting and digging, to let them run and work and experiment, sleep, have regular meals, the sights and sounds of winter and spring, autumn and summer, birds, and the near presence of mothers.
Margaret McMillan,
***The Camp School*, 1917**

The essential ingredient was for children to learn with adult support and interaction. For example, if playing with blocks to talk about the colours, sizes, shapes, why one tower fell over and another stayed upright, and so on. Today adults put equipment out and watch children play without using opportunities for learning.

Rosemary Allday
(Student 1959 - 62)

ment and garden on the wasteland site. Small children would wander in awe among the fennel, mint, lavender, sage, marjoram, thyme, rosemary and rue, that had been planted in the herb garden "pinching the leaves with their tiny fingers and then putting their tiny fingers to their noses… to them the tall bed of marjoram is a blooming field. Their little heads do not reach as high as the fennel. Coming back with odorous hands… their eyes are bright, their mouths open."

Margaret McMillan was keen to introduce and utilise new educational methods for the teaching of the pre-school children who attended the Baby Camp. She had made extensive trips abroad to observe the experimental work of other educationalists and had extensively studied the work and writings of Fredrich Froebel and Edouard Seguin among others. She drew upon some of their ideas and introduced them to the camp. She had come to believe that children should be nurtured and encouraged with love and

kindness to think for themselves and to learn through the freedom of play. The traditionally approved methods of teaching were a far cry from these radical theories. Those young children who attended the infant departments of Board Schools were used to hard benches, repressive teaching regimes and the cane. Margaret McMillan and her staff quickly saw that their new charges associated teachers with the cane, hiding their hands behind their backs out of habit whenever they saw a teacher. The children seemed at first bewildered at their new-found liberty. The freedom to move, play and freely experience the open space of the camp was alien to them. The parents, too, needed reassurance as to the benefits the Baby Camp could offer. Many parents sewed their offspring into their clothes during the winter months and it took a long time for Margaret McMillan to gain their confidence and persuade them that the children would benefit from daily washing at the camp.

The outbreak of the First World War provided Margaret McMillan with the opportunity to develop further her work with pre-school children. Large numbers of local women were required for work in the munitions factories in Woolwich. So that these women could be released to do this work the Ministry of Munitions authorised a childcare allowance of seven pence a day for very young children. The McMillans opened up the Baby Camp to these children and, in doing so, began to form what would eventually become the Rachel McMillan Nursery School. Pre-school children attended the Baby Camp, while the older boys and girls who had previously been living at the Night Camps now jointly used the camp site across the road during the day. The night attendance at the camp had to be abandoned on account of air raids and the difficulty of finding night guardians.

Staff for the Baby Camp were also in short supply and many different people were engaged to help run it. Often these were girls who had just left school or those who had been ill and were advised to work in the open air. Others were retired nurses and teachers. The main running of the camp was left to Rachel, as Margaret often travelled the country giving lectures.

Situated in the midst of the air raid danger zone, the work of the Baby Camp was often disrupted by German Zeppelin raids. During this time Rachel and Margaret both lived in the small house on the Baby Camp site. In August 1916, the McMillans were victims of one such raid. Afterwards Margaret developed septicæmia and had to be gradually nursed back to health by Rachel.

The pressures of running the camp and clinic, nursing Margaret and living in various lodgings after the destruction of their house, proved too much. Rachel McMillan succumbed to exhaustion and illness, dying on her birthday, 25 March 1917. A very small funeral, attended by some of the camp children who had bought a small

[Rachel] came into the room where I was asleep. "Those troublesome Zeps again!" she said lightly. The room was ablaze with a wicked light. A moment later, and while I was getting up the window crashed in… The house shook as three terrible blasts followed one another in quick succession. The last bomb, fallen only fifty yards off, tore up the iron work of the frontage and threw it in on the floor… the windows and sashes fell in, and an acrid smell filled the house… We went from the house, now filled with poisonous gas, and took refuge for the night in the babies' pavilion.

Margaret's description of the Zeppelin raid on the night of 27 August 1916.

wreath with their little savings, took place in the cemetery at Brockley.

Margaret was devastated and it was many months before the shock began to subside. Even then, she would always be deeply affected by her sister's death, coming to believe that Rachel was at her side guiding and giving her the strength to continue: "[Rachel] was the moving spirit through all the confusion of our lives", she later recalled.

Margaret McMillan decided to honour her sister's memory by renaming the Baby Camp and establishing a training institution. Characteristically, she announced the changes, one morning in 1918, by affixing a notice to the Baby Camp entrance that read: The Rachel McMillan Memorial Training Centre and Open-Air Nursery School. "I have called the Baby Camp by her name" she wrote, "so that all who may see it will remember her by this saying 'educate every child as if he were your own'."

With this in mind, Margaret McMillan devoted the rest of her life to establishing the Nursery School and Training Centre in Deptford.

The Rachel McMillan Memorial Training College & Nursery School

Shortly after Rachel's funeral, a friend left Margaret McMillan a legacy of £1,200 and she used it to rebuild the shelter that had been damaged during the war, ignoring the fact that her tenure was terminable at a day's notice. Since occupying the site she had had several shelters constructed. In August 1917, Mr H A L Fisher, the President of the Board of Education, was invited to open the new building. In the same year Margaret McMillan was awarded the CBE in recognition of her work, and she published her book *The Camp School*.

H A L Fisher's Education Act 1918 empowered local authorities to establish nursery school and class provision and also aid voluntary nursery schools like Margaret McMillan's. Even so the Nursery School would not benefit from any financial help until 1920, so Margaret McMillan had to run everything on donations, private subscriptions, and the residue of the Ministry of Munitions grant which had ceased at the end of the war.

The LCC finally recognised the Rachel McMillan Nursery School, giving it its first grant in September 1920, after making an agreement with Margaret McMillan over the future of the Stowage site. She would be allowed to continue with the project on the condition that upon her death the site and all its property would revert back to the control of the LCC.

The Nursery School, now LCC grant aided, had to abide by the Board of Education ruling that only children between the ages of two and five were eligible for the grant. Babies under two were removed to a nearby day nursery, and those over five either moved over the road to the Camp School or started at primary school. This caused great distress to Margaret McMillan, who believed that children should not be moved to primary school until they were at least seven years old. But the Board of Education was adamant that only children between two and five

[The Nursery School] did not duplicate the features of the home, it remedied its features. There were no baths in the children's homes; there were numerous baths at the shelters. There was no hot water in the homes; there was an abundant and constant supply at the school. The homes were stuffy and sordid; the school was bright and clean, and open to the sunshine and the four winds.

Margaret McMillan,
The Nursery School

My mother took me along to see Miss McMillan when I was just 2 years old. She greeted me with open arms and insisted I stayed for the day. I 'stayed' there for over 13 years! My school days were truly some of the happiest of my life, and when I left, I wept.

Dorothy Adshead
(Pupil 1916 - 26)

Queen Mary visits Deptford, 1919

would receive the grant – the others would have to be removed. So Margaret McMillan continued to educate 50 or 60 older children in the Camp School, relying upon what families could afford to pay, along with donations from friends and those interested in the project. Even so the Camp School would always remain the poor relation to the Nursery School and Training Centre.

Meanwhile, the Nursery School was overflowing. In 1919 there had been 40 children in attendance, rising to 135 by the summer of 1921. Staff were turning away parents on a daily basis. The waiting list for the Nursery School was very long. McMillan had been elected as member of the LCC for Deptford in 1919 and, as "one of those awkward people who want things done", she approached her fellow LCC members with a proposal for an extension to the nursery. The LCC went ahead, building its own shelters on the site for another one hundred children. The two nurseries merged under the management of Margaret McMillan and were run as one school. Queen Mary, who had first visited the nursery in 1919, was invited back to open the two new shelters on 22 November 1921, and she maintained an active interest in the Nursery School and Training Centre until the 1960s, often making official visits and occasionally donating money.

By 1922 the number of children attending the nursery had risen to 212. The newcomers that arrived, led there by their mothers or older siblings, would appear at the nursery gates having been subdued with a lump of bread and jam or sticky toffee apples, often unsuitably clothed – heavy in summer and flimsy in winter.

Rickets was the most common defect among the new toddlers. Absorbed into the Nursery School life, fed on oatmeal, fresh fruit and vegetables, the miraculous change in their physical and general development was obvious. Over a period of two years Margaret McMillan recorded over 70 cures in rickety children. When it came to the great influenza epidemic of December 1921, however, the new children did not fare so well. Attendance at the Nursery on the last day before the Christmas break numbered 184: when it reopened only 131 children returned. Though there were no deaths among those children who had been there the longest, it was the new children who had not built up enough immunity that died. Outside the school hundreds of children died.

The Nursery School day was a long one, from 8 am to 5.30 pm. Margaret McMillan urged the necessity of this long 'nurture' day in order to combat the sufferings of the children. She stressed that the Nursery School was not a copy of the home; its main function would be to compensate for all that home failed to provide.

The open shelters, nestling among the maturing garden of herbs, flowers, vegetables and at least twenty different varieties of trees, must have seemed like paradise to the small children who arrived through the Nursery gates. "From the beginning" wrote Margaret McMillan, the Nursery School was "a garden school. Not a house with a garden attached, but a garden furnished with light… shelters… with trees."

The Nursery School was furnished with child-sized tables and chairs, all made by the staff or local craftspeople. The garden paths, steps and terraces were child-orientated also. There were little wooden play houses and a 'Jungle Jim' climbing frame designed by Margaret McMillan herself.

She also made a special feature of animals, keeping goats, chickens, cats, pigeons, rabbits, guinea pigs and mice, and an aviary of bright yellow canaries. The children rarely saw animals outside the nursery, so living among these creatures must have been a wonderful experience. McMillan saw all the features of the Garden School as necessities, noting that "they are even more necessary than apparatus. Human beings did not become human in prisons and cellars."

The garden and the 'Jungle Jim'

[Miss McMillan] wanted her children to enjoy the freedom of water, running water. Bathing the under-fives who came from very bad homes (a tap in the yard) was part of the nursery school day. 'Juniors' had shower baths as well as little wash basins and the children did really get running water all over.

Mary Peet (Student 1929 - 32)

The 'nurture' day would begin with the bathing of the children. Bathrooms were attached to each shelter. The two year olds had individual bath tubs raised up on platforms so that the staff would not strain their backs. The older children had a large bath at floor level in which several children were bathed at the same time. The children were encouraged to see bathing as a pleasant experience. Bathing could be an educational instrument as well as a hygienic one. She developed her theories of touch training around the activity of bathing. By insisting on regular washing she helped the children become aware of differences of temperature, the movement of the water and the feel of fabric against their skin. After bathing each would be dressed in clean clothing and an embroidered overall of pink or blue. Their hair would be brushed and the girls would have brightly coloured ribbons tied in their hair.

The children took all their meals at the Nursery School. Parents were expected to pay unless they were unable to afford it. A breakfast of Scottish porridge was served at nine. A two course dinner followed at twelve o'clock, and at four, a meal of brown bread, honey and milk with either cake or fruit was provided.

During the rest of the day time was spent playing, dancing, drawing, making and listening to music, storytelling and sleeping. There were tables that ran along the sides of the shelter walls where educational apparatus could be freely found: bright coloured discs and balls, wooden letters to fit into puzzles, pictures and picture books. All these toys were designed to help the children develop their skills in recognising size, shape and colour. Margaret McMillan developed the 'Wonder Bag' for the younger children. These draw-string bags contained shapes and objects which the children were encouraged to take out and look at, feel and smell. There were wall boards where children could stand and chalk pictures or the beginnings of letters and numbers. Music was played on the piano or gramophone and the children invited to join in with singing or dancing. They could freely wander the garden observing the flowers and trees, touching and stroking the many animals that lived there.

Children who had reached the age of four were encouraged to explore the early stages of reading and numbers. Those who were younger were encouraged to talk and observe. No child was ever pressed into continuing with an activity in which they had lost interest. Most importantly, the children were allowed to express themselves freely, to say what they felt, to try to say what they meant. No child would have ever been told 'you must not speak'. Margaret McMillan recalled how, one afternoon in the nursery: "one little boy was making a hideous noise. 'That's not like a little boy – to make a noise like that!' [I] said gently. 'I'm not a little boy!' he replied, 'I'm a motorcar – I'm skidding.' That taught me a lesson... he could not have told

me what he was doing if he had been afraid of me. Only when we get fear away, do we begin to get anything."

Even though the work of the Nursery and the Camp Schools went a long way to broaden the horizons of the children, Margaret McMillan was troubled that many of the children had never been to the countryside or even seen the sea. So she arranged with the Principal of Avery Hill Training College in 1923 for 80 children to spend two weeks of the summer in one of the college hostels. The holiday was such a success that it was the first of many holidays for the children away from the streets of Deptford. Friends and supporters began to offer their country homes during the summer months. Even the Dowager Countess of Warwick, a close friend of Edward VII and a convert to socialism, invited a group of children to her home at Easton Lodge for three weeks. The children were so well-behaved that the butler declared he preferred them to trade unionists any day.

The Wonder Bag & Gramophone

Wonderful holidays at the Margaret McMillan House, Wrotham, Kent. Such fun we had, collecting the milk from the local farm, going for long walks over the Downs, playing in the woods that surrounded the Home...
Lily Lynn (Pupil 1929 - 38)

Despite all the kind offers of holidays for the children, Margaret McMillan still longed for a country house which she could use as a holiday camp year after year. Sadly, this did not happen until after her death, when a legacy left by Lettuce Floyd, a committed suffragette and McMillan supporter, was used to build Margaret McMillan House at Wrotham, Kent. This house was used as a holiday home for both the Nursery and Camp School children, until the outbreak of the Second World War. It is now owned by the Margaret McMillan Field Studies Centre Trust and, under the management of Greenwich Council, continues to provide local children with educational holidays.

Spreading the Word

Margaret McMillan was very proud of what had been achieved at the Nursery School and never once missed an opportunity to further its cause. She regularly invited and welcomed visits by many prominent and influential people. No-one would be able to resist an invitation from Margaret McMillan for very long. George Bernard Shaw *[pictured right]* was one of those pressed into paying a visit to her "lovely brats" as he called them. Dora and Bertrand Russell visited, as did Stanley Baldwin, the Prime Minister. One visit proved particularly fortunate, in that it led to the eventual construction of the Rachel McMillan Training Centre. A Mrs Wintingham, who visited the Nursery School in 1924, was so impressed that she persuaded her friend, the Conservative MP Lady Nancy Astor, to help secure the future of the Training Centre and Nursery School. Lady Astor gave her whole-hearted support to Margaret McMillan's work, and from this developed a

When Prime Minister Stanley Baldwin came to our school, [Miss McMillan] was so charming to him and so determined he should miss nothing. I can see her now linking her arm in his. I knew she cared little for his politics, it rather amused me at the time! It was always a proud moment for her when she was 'showing us off' to her celebrated visitors.
Dorothy Lob (Pupil, 1920s)

Life in those early days of the College was very exciting. One never knew what famous person one would meet in the children's shelters or at the simple meals served in the 'Memorial Room'. I remember most clearly Rudolph Steiner, grave and impressive, and Lady Astor, laughing and skipping around with the children.
Margaret Lamming (Student 1923 - 25)

Rachel McMillan Training College, opened in 1930 by Queen Mary [ABOVE], and the Training College Library [BELOW]

devoted friendship between the two women, much to the surprise of Margaret McMillan's socialist friends and supporters.

News of the Nursery School and its work had spread far and wide. Its good reputation had also begun to attract interest from those who wished to train as teachers and nursery workers. Margaret McMillan had always believed that if her work was to be secured, it would be necessary to equip and train an army of nursery workers, who could eventually go on to establish hundreds of Open-Air Nursery Schools across the country. In 1919 she had begun to organise the formal training of students within the school. In the same year the Board of Education officially recognised the Nursery School as a training centre for certified teachers and nursery workers. There were initially twenty student nursery workers living in four local hostels, among the children and families with whom they worked. Most students came from middle class backgrounds, and many were shocked when they first encountered the squalor and poverty of Deptford.

The training course syllabus was divided into three areas. Each student was expected to spend three hours per day working in the nursery and also observe and help in the clinic. Practical courses were held on voice production and drama, drawing, pottery and primitive arts, decorative design, making toys and nursery apparatus, singing and gardening. The third aspect involved lectures on educational methods, English or history, physiology and hygiene, and on the methods and apparatus of the McMillan School.

The Rachel McMillan Training Centre continued to grow and to attract attention. Many prospective students were seeking admission and it became clear that a purpose-built centre with accommodation would have to be found for the students. In 1928 Margaret McMillan set about raising the funds to build the new college building. Lord Astor was persuaded to purchase the land in Creek Road. Lady Astor raised £20,000 for the building and in November 1929 laid the foundation stone. The new building was completed in the spring of 1930 and Queen Mary was invited to open the new college. The work of Margaret McMillan was acknowledged when in the same year as the opening of the new college she was awarded the Companion of Honour, arriving at Buckingham Palace in a new black lace dress with the hem held up with a safety pin!

I remember asking [Miss McMillan], a keen Socialist, why she had asked Queen Mary to open the new College, "It's for my children", she said. What a day it was (8 May 1930) with a feeling of spring. All the children wore clean overalls and a shoe firm provided new sandals. The garden was bright and gay with flowers (some buried in their pots and taken up the next day). A very steady-handed student served Queen Mary with tea in the new dining room.
Mary Peet (Student 1929 - 32)

My last picture of [Miss McMillan] is of the afternoon before she died. She looked calm and peaceful as I sat holding her hand. She looked up and in a very quiet voice she said "Look after my children". I felt a very heavy burden laid on me.

Alice Campbell (Head of Baby Camp & Nursery School 1925 - 45)

The Death of Margaret McMillan

Towards the end of 1930 Margaret McMillan was taken ill and moved to a nursing home in Harrow where she died on 27 March 1931. She was laid to rest next to her sister Rachel in Brockley cemetery. In recognition of her work, the councils of Deptford and Greenwich erected a memorial to her in the garden of the Nursery School *[pictured left]* placing it appropriately near the bungalow where she had lived among the children.

Margaret McMillan's contribution to education was unique in its emphasis on the duty of society to provide 'nurture' (both physical and mental) to young, growing human beings. Her true concern for the whole function and process of early years education was revealed in a interview recorded for the BBC in 1927. After describing a typical Nursery School day with its adventure, movement, food and rest, its music, dancing, and talking, she continued: "You may ask, why should we give all this to the children? Because this is nurture, and without it they can never really have education. For education must grow out of nurture as the flower from its root, since nurture is organic; it is the right building up of nerve structure and brain cell... Much of the money we spend on education is wasted because we have not laid any real foundation for our education system... The education system should grow out of the Nursery School system, not out of a neglected infancy."

THE McMILLAN ETHOS
by Emily Adlington

Margaret McMillan campaigned on many issues, including school medical inspection, school baths and free school meals but she is most famously remembered for her contribution to early years education.

At the centre of her ethos was the belief that all children have immense potential and all must be given the best possible educational environment to achieve this. McMillan's life was spurred by a vision of a future state in which children would not grow up in crowded slums where disease and death were rife, a future in which all would have freedom to grow and learn without struggling to break out of the cycles of disadvantage.

This was a vision driven by a Christian socialism that convinced her that everyone, including young children, needed the chance of education and the chance to make a difference in society.

A Garden of Children

Margaret McMillan's idea of the nursery school was centred around the garden. Her own early childhood memories are full of description about the garden of the house her family lived in whilst in America. This happy childhood image was shattered by the death of her father and her younger sister, Elizabeth, when Margaret was five. In this sense the garden is, for Margaret, not only a place where joyful times are remembered but a place of her own emotional restoration. It is said that the shelters of the open-air nursery in Deptford resemble the house in America, which she described: "The wooden house is a mere shelter in summer, with long wide-open windows that are like doors opening on the stoep (veranda). It seems less a house than a kind of roofed series of gateways opening on the wide sunlit world."

Anyone who has visited the Rachel McMillan Nursery School could describe the shelters in very similar

The garden meant so much to Miss McMillan and indeed to all of us at Deptford. To open the gate in the wooden palings along Church Street and to enter there was to pass from one world to another. The streets were lined mainly with shabby houses, pubs and little shops. But on the other side of the gate was the garden — flowers, and the mulberry tree at the far end, and the children in bright coloured overalls were playing there...
Gladys Harvey (Student 1918)

You may make a garden anywhere – in a back street, in slum areas, near railway bridges, and where life is dark. You may find your gardeners also everywhere.
Margaret McMillan, 'In Our Garden: An Experiment with Teddy'
***The Christian World*, 27 March 1913**

terms. Building nursery gardens may have been a symbol of Margaret's vision of what she had lost and yet could offer to children who otherwise may have had very little access to nature.

Margaret's vision of a garden of children was not purely based on her own childhood memories. She saw the educational importance of the garden and actively sought to provide a curriculum that met the all-round needs of a child. Margaret was very well read in many of the educational, philosophical and scientific ideas of the day. Her work bears traces of influence from many famous theorists, including Seguin, Froebel, Owen, Plato and Rousseau. She was able to take what she learnt from others and adapt it to her own vision and work.

In the symbol of the garden, it is the influence of Fredrich Froebel which is most striking. Margaret McMillan was an active member of the Froebel Society for a number of years and his name appeared in many of her speeches and writings. In a speech to the Froebel Society in Bradford, McMillan explained that she had been drawn to the society because Froebel had expressed the need for the child to be close to nature. She referred to him as "the champion of the poor" since his idea of the garden of children was primarily a dream for slum children. McMillan was very impressed by the Froebel school in Kensington when she visited it in 1899: "Into the cool, quiet corridors of the bright spacious rooms the morning sun shone brightly. The parquetted floors, the wooden walls, the softly-coloured ceiling, were the framework of a tranquil and harmonised environment where the needs of the sub-conscious life were abundantly recognised. For the young child the tone is more than the word, the colour and the light is more than the lesson book, the sights and sounds and contacts of the school are the influences that mould him…"

The description shows how McMillan developed her views on the importance of sensory learning years before setting up the nursery school in Deptford. On the same visit she was also encouraged by the fact that the children and teachers alike appeared to be learning through 'life'. The teachers were learning about botany, zoology, biology and psychology in order to understand about life, its various forms and its nature. Children learn through the senses; they learn through life. This organic understanding of learning strongly influenced Margaret McMillan and impressed upon her the importance of using natural materials in teaching.

Froebel spoke often of the 'child-garden' and saw each child as an 'organic unity'. However, although he saw the importance of colour, air and large movement, the 'child-garden' is not necessarily a physical garden. Rather it is a philosophical conception of the links between the child and the world in which he or she develops. McMillan saw the 'child-garden' in a remarkably similar way. Only she saw it as a vision

In little children [McMillan] saw the early seeds of power; not to get on in the world, but to live in beauty. She knew that freedom in the right environment, with a spiritual dynamic, would bring out all that was good and true in the little ones, whose imaginations and questionings were free and unfettered.
Dr Albert Mansbridge, Speech at Commemoration Service, 1950

[43]

Students were responsible for caring for the various pets: canaries and budgerigars in the aviary, doves in the dovecot, guinea pigs, rabbits, and hens, and — last but by no means the least important — Daisy the goat, who mischievously enjoyed butting the more timid student as she tried to tether her on grass under the mulberry tree.

Honor Edwards (Student 1923 - 25)

that must become a physical reality.

Building on the idea that each child is an organic unity, Margaret held to the philosophy that a child, and indeed a person of any age, needs to be able to develop as a whole. Physical, spiritual, intellectual, social and emotional development are intrinsically linked. There must be links between one's spiritual nature and physical work. In an article for the *Labour Prophet* in 1895, McMillan quoted Froebel as saying "Religion, without work, is apt to degenerate into empty dreaming and purposeless emotion, while on the other hand, work without religion tends to degrade man into a machine."

Therefore, her garden was to be a place in which children would not only discover scientific facts, learn to count, and begin to talk about what they saw, but a place in which children could discover their inner selves and allow learning to flow from that. The garden is a place of social community in which the child must find his or her

place. Not only was the child to be seen organically but the educational environment itself was an organic unity. Practically, the ideal physical environment in which to offer this was an Open-Air Nursery.

The Rachel McMillan Nursery School, opened in 1914, can be seen as having four main emphases: nurture, appropriate education, parent and community involvement, and specialist early years training.

Nurture

Margaret McMillan's emphasis on nurture in early education meant that every aspect of a child's being must be loved and catered for. At the foundation of this lay the child's physical well-being. In 1910 disease and sickness were rife in the slums of Deptford and most families lived in extremely cramped conditions, exacerbating the problems. McMillan saw that poverty, disease and a lack of hygiene were enemies to education. A child who is undernourished or sick simply can not learn to her or his full potential. Margaret and Rachel worked hard to enable the children to learn in an environment that was hygienic and ensured healthy diet and lots of fresh air. Fresh air was seen as a part of bettering the health of the slum child and the McMillans proved this to be a good cure. In order for children to receive the necessary physical care most children attended the nursery for a nine-hour day. Although in much of her writing McMillan sometimes appears to over-emphasise specific instructions on physical care, her belief that a happy child was a healthy child is one that few would debate. Margaret believed that caring for the physical should naturally lead to all-round nurture. Ultimately, she saw nurture as loving and educating each child as your own. Physical care was a basis for learning. In her book *Early Childhood* (1901) Margaret McMillan wrote that the role of primary teachers was "to offer good nourishment and to create a desire for it." Children are themselves part of the organic nature of the garden, needing to be fed and watered not just physically but intellectually, socially, emotionally and spiritually. A child who is offered good nourishment in a suitable environment will usually respond by actively seeking learning for themselves.

Appropriate Education

If nurture encourages natural learning, how should an appropriate educational curriculum be developed? Margaret McMillan thought it preferable that children remained in the nursery environment until at least the age of seven. This was due to her understanding of the need for a child to develop freely and the importance of a child-centred curriculum that caters for the whole child.

The basis of an appropriate education must be an appropriately planned environment. Margaret McMillan wrote at great length as to how a garden can be planned to provide necessary learning experiences. Take a

Where was there a school where the children were showered with so much love? What fun we had at Christmas parties — magic man and presents. The many outings Miss McMillan took us on, visits to the Old Vic, Tower of London, British Museum, Albert Hall, besides many others. She would bundle as many of us as possible into a taxi. We were packed like sardines, but it was always great fun.
Dorothy Lob (Pupil 1920s)

Equality does not begin in the school. It begins in the nursery. The word has gone forth: "Nurture for all".
Margaret McMillan, *What the Open-Air Nursery School Is*, 1923

To us [Miss McMillan] was all-powerful, we could face anybody or anything with her beside us.
I can still hear her saying — you may be poor now but if you want to, there is nothing to stop you sitting in the Houses of Parliament.
Gladys Woodhams (Pupil, 1920s)

Learning outdoors – McMillan
style table activities

garden with trees, flowers, animals, plants, grass, walls, walkways, greenhouse, steps, herbs, vegetables. Add to it sandpits, water, climbing frames, slides, bikes, building materials, art materials and other educational apparatus, and there is a wealth of learning opportunity. Literacy, number, creativity, care for others and other such lessons can all be provided outdoors.

Most striking about the McMillan idea of learning in the garden is her description of how the garden can capture a child's imagination through the senses. She believed that the outdoor environment, "the freedom of nature", brought about "an appeal of life" that catches the senses and awakens learning. Free play in the garden fostered sensory development, bringing a "natural excitement" to learning. Teaching that does not allow children to learn freely can be damaging. "Formal teaching will never take place of experience." Rather than being taught by rote, children ought to be free to explore the environment and learn to make discoveries for themselves. Margaret McMillan saw the imagination as a power that "lights up all work" and "gives life and meaning" to activities. Therefore, for education to capture a child's imagination is vital if learning is to have life and meaning. She pointed out that imagination cannot simply be given to a child through a teacher but teachers can learn to foster it through imaginative planning and careful direction. Imagination at an early age is often captured through art and, since nature exemplifies art, its colours, sounds, smells, textures and movements have a power to reach the imagination through sensory experience. For example, a young child may be fascinated by the smooth feeling of a fistful of sand disappearing through the fingers. As a result she becomes a researcher who begins to understand gravity and volume. Also, natural curiosity may lead to discussion and new vocabulary. This reveals McMillan's philosophy of education as recognising the importance of *processes* before *outcomes*. The process works as follows: Nature captures the senses and the imagination. This leads to inquisitiveness (play and research) which may involve physical skills, language, social skills, reasoning, assimilation and accommodation – resulting in learning.

We cannot expect any pre-school child to reach certain targets or stages of learning without first considering the importance of the learning environment and the value of empowering a child to seek learning for himself. Early education must allow children to explore through the senses before expecting measurable learning to occur.

Although Margaret McMillan stressed that every part of an early years curriculum can be carried out in the garden, this vision had to be grounded in the reality of the weather. The shelters, therefore, were built in continuity with the garden. McMillan described the shelters as being organic themselves. "I can best describe the buildings by saying that they are adjustable – they have what corresponds to sensitiveness in an organism. The walls can be darkened, or thickened; they can be opened in part; they can be removed altogether."

She also spoke of the need for inside to be light, spacious and planned to give a sense of "sweet freedom". The importance of everything being open to change within the context of careful planning highlights McMillan's philosophy that everyone and everything has the ability to grow and become better. Miriam Lord recalled Margaret McMillan placing a tiny seed in her hand and saying "never forget the potentiality of a seed". Our ability to grow physically exemplifies that growth of every kind is implicit in human nature. According to Margaret McMillan, growth is "a revelation... there is nothing in the man that is not implicit in the little child, and... there should be nothing in the higher school or university that is not implicit in the nursery school."

As I walked down the whole length of Church Street I was profoundly shocked and depressed by what I saw – the squalid poverty, the dilapidated buildings, the sickly children playing listlessly in the street. There were women nursing babies on their doorsteps and men lounging against walls.

Then I came to the tall wooden gate of the Rachel McMillan Nursery School... and passed through it to what seemed a veritable paradise. The contrast was overwhelming. A beautiful spacious garden, trees, grass, flowers, sunshine and brilliant colour lifted up my heart and dispelled depression.

The whole place seemed to be swarming with happy, healthy little children all dressed in bright overalls of every hue. Among the children was Miss McMillan with her crown of silver gold hair, her imposing presence, simple dignity and kindly greeting. I knew that here was a truly great woman...
Honor Edwards
(Student 1923 - 25, Staff 1925 - 31)

The child of the city appears at first a little bewildered by his new found liberty. But he accustoms himself quickly … I have seen two three-year-olds career down and up the wide pavilion for half an hour, naked, and forgetting everything but the joy of running.
Margaret McMillan
***The Camp School*, 1917**

To dreamers of a new world [McMillan] points out that, in the continuous accession of children, a new world is always being born, and, through our mistreatment of them, always being lost.
'The Portrait Gallery'
***The Woman Worker*, 5 June 1908**

Miss McMillan was the founder of the Parents & Teachers Association as they are now known. In Deptford she invited the parents at regular intervals to have tea and biscuits and meet the teachers and students. How the mothers enjoyed this – away for an hour or so from their over-crowded homes.
Gwen Yorath (Student 1920 - 23)

Early education must, therefore, value all forms of activity and encourage growth to the extent of each individual's full potential.

Parental & Community Involvement

Parent involvement in the nursery was very important to Margaret. She felt strongly that nursery education should be an extension and benefit to home not a replacement of it. Without the parents as partners in a child's education the nursery is not a true nursery, it becomes a mere receiving station. She actively sought to involve parents in the school and communicate with them about their child's development. Margaret also saw that the nursery could be a place of learning for parents and other adults. She especially wanted adults to see how important children were, that they must be seen as precious first-rate citizens as opposed to troublesome beings at the bottom of the social system. Involving the parents in their child's education helped to foster greater interest and a sense of

parental responsibility as opposed to apathetic acceptance of whatever the staff thought and did.

Beyond the immediate families, the local community was also important. Community runs as a thread through Margaret McMillan's work, and she saw this as operating at a number of different levels. Within the nursery, children belonged to a certain shelter – these were seen as providing small units to promote a secure environment and an immediate structure in which to develop socially. Children ate, slept and carried out certain activities in these groups. Then came the nursery as a whole, staff and children. Next the community with the parents and families of the children and, beyond this, the community of Deptford. Not only did she want the children to learn about different people and the community of Deptford, she wanted the nursery to be seen as a part of Deptford and for everyone to learn about the importance of early childhood. Hence,

Margaret saw the nursery as a place that ought to work not only for the good of the children but for the development of the whole community.

Early Years Training

Originally part of the Nursery itself, from 1930, specialist staff training had its own building. The Rachel McMillan Training College was immediately next door to the Nursery giving students plenty of practical experience and exposure to McMillanism at work. Training, in this context, offered opportunities for students to develop intellectually as well as learning about young children.

McMillan was clear that what she was doing in Deptford may not necessarily work well in other contexts. She wanted her training to teach students about child development. They would learn to observe for themselves the needs of early childhood and consider how these might best be met. Inevitably, students would be influenced by the routine and activities at the Nursery School. However, other communities may well have different specific needs and it was stressed that nursery provision ought to meet these.

McMillanism is not a prescriptive theory. Although she was adamant that the garden provides the best environment for learning and that curriculum must be carefully planned to cater for all-round child development, her wider philosophy is one of growth, processes, change and care for each individual. These principles, in combination with observation and planning, ought to guide a teacher's work.

Margaret McMillan's influence in early years training was world-wide. Many international students came to receive training at the Rachel McMillan college. Abigail Elist came to the college in 1921, sent by the Women's Education Association of Boston with a view to starting a nursery school there on her return. Describing her training she wrote: "We students worked a part of each day with the children. I remember that there were three shifts of

The cardinal sins of the leaders in education of this country have been sins against the involuntary and of the subconscious – sins against the power of emotion as the sustainer of all vigorous, mental and moral life.

Our examination halls are crowded with young people who can answer questions on Staff Notation, but who have no real love of music, who 'get up' geography and can tell you the exact height of various mountains, but who have no appreciation of the beauty of the wood that overshadows their own city, or the stream that winds through their own glen. They learn history, and take amazing pains to commit to memory a great many dates and lists of kings, with the names of battles and treaties. Such knowledge is very well – only it has no roots. It is fixed and nourished by no personal elements. Kept green by no sweet well-spring of emotion.

Margaret McMillan,
The Ethical End in Education,
c.1900

"Brown bread, always brown bread", remembered Peggy Shade, a pupil at the nursery in the 1920s

us in the long day from 7 am to 6 pm. We helped to give each child a bath every other day and sometimes hair was washed. We dressed the children every day in bright smocks, combed their hair, tying the girls with bright ribbons. We helped to serve the three meals which were given, and to supervise the long afternoon nap; to guide their hand-work and play both in the shelter and outside it in the garden. By actual work, guided by the skillful teacher's example and suggestion, we learned what young children could do, what help they needed, what attitude toward them brought the best results, what makes up a young child's day. We were involved in their learning and their physical welfare and development... Devoted care, fresh air, food, sleep and interesting things to do for a long happy day – this was the recipe laid down by Miss McMillan. It entailed hard work and long hours with large numbers of children; but the children gained and the students' eyes were opened... Miss McMillan and

other teachers gave us students lectures. My memory of these is dim except for the atmosphere Miss McMillan created. She was clearly a personage as she lectured and conveyed to us her convictions both positive and negative. Out of her intuition and experience, buttressed by her creativeness and indomitable will, she knew what the nursery school should be and do and what was good for little children. Such sincerity, self-confidence and commitment, as bit by bit we understood it, was unforgettable. 'Treat every child as if he were your own'."

Abigail Elist opened the Ruggles Street Nursery School and Training Centre in Boston on 1 January 1922. From this many other Nursery Schools were opened across the United States and Canada. Abigail Elist wrote that her time in Deptford "laid the foundation" on which all her work was based. Margaret McMillan and other teachers gave her "an eagerness and a confidence which I have kept throughout the years". Thus from small beginnings the work and ethos of Margaret McMillan had a profound effect on the beginnings on the Nursery School movement in America.

Another example of Margaret's world-wide influence is in India. In an article in 1960, Leila da Costa wrote of the way that McMillanism influenced early years education in India:

'The name of Margaret McMillan dominates a brilliant group of educational entrepreneurs who changed the focus of first British, then Indian, child education... Indeed, Nursery School education and Margaret McMillan were synonymous terms in India in the late twenties of this country... In the later part of the twenties and early thirties Indian women, students of the Rachel McMillan Training College in Deptford, returned to their country inspired with the experience of that first Nursery School and Training College devoted to the cause of the child under five... As a result of direct training in Deptford or indirectly by studying the McMillan sisters' writings on this subject... educationalists and prominent social workers began to study this question of the necessity of Nursery Schools.

The Nursery School, as we conceive it in India has a three-fold mission: First to take charge of the child's physical life and in effect to reproduce the healthy conditions of a nursery in a well-managed home, and provide an environment in which the health of the young child – physical, mental, moral – can be safe-guarded. Secondly, a good Nursery School is a source of education and its success depends upon the ability of the teacher to create a living community in which the babies develop their senses and imagination. Thirdly, allied to this function, is the social purpose underlying it – children acquire, under wise superintendence, a right personal and communal behaviour...

The rapid growth of pre-primary education in an organised basis on a national scale (in India) was based

The daily living conditions [for the students] were hard and somewhat bleak. The four local Hostels in four different Deptford streets were set in the local community in Albury Street, Evelyn Street, King Street and Wellington Street, and we were often kept awake at night by drunken brawls in and around the local pubs.
Honor Edwards (Student 1923 - 25, Staff 1925 - 31)

I remember... going over the road from College to Wellington Street Hostel each night, and using the outdoor bathroom in fear and trembling because of the explosive geysers!
Winifred Bonny (Student 1925 - 28)

The girls looked particularly gay in their overalls with large bows of ribbon tying up their hair. One of our jobs was ironing the ribbons each night. Wide and colourful they were and I suppose the hot iron killed most of the lice...
Mary Peet (Student 1929 - 32)

Children discover the world through play. Teachers' input should be interactive not interrupting.

directly on the teaching of the McMillan sisters. A large number of the members of this select committee had first hand experience of the teachings and practice of the Misses McMillan."

Leila da Costa went on to describe some of the nursery education and training colleges that were set up and influenced by the work in Deptford. In 1960 there were at least a dozen co-educational training schools in West Bengal and it was estimated that about 100 students were trained each year and went out to teach in village schools. "Thus in an indirect and diluted fashion even the remotest village school in West Bengal will benefit from the teachings of Margaret McMillan – the pioneer of nursery education in the UK and the inspirer of nursery schools even today. It is not wishful thinking to hope that perhaps one of the little girls learning to use her limbs and enjoying the atmosphere of the Nursery School in one of these villages, will one day, when grown to womanhood, visit the

Nursery School and Training College at Deptford and learn again what Margaret McMillan did for unborn children of many lands when she started her first school clinic at Bow in 1908 and her first Nursery school at Deptford in 1911.

Tagore wrote of such as her 'Thou hast made me known to friends whom I knew not. Thou hast given me seats in homes not my own'."

Margaret McMillan was a fighter. Her enemies were ignorance, prejudice, dirt and disease. She said "to be weak is to be wicked; to stand still is to go back". Her last message to her students was: "Tell my girls to stick to the slums. Many teachers can be found for the schools set in pleasant places. The bravest and best are needed for the slums."
Emma Stevinson,
***Rachel McMillan Training College Newsletter*, July 1931**

When [Miss McMillan] was given the Freedom of the Borough of Deptford, the golden key was kept in a glass case which hung on the wall of the dining room and, on either side of a large portrait of Rachel McMillan, was inscribed in beautiful lettering... a motto attributed to King Alfred: "I desire to live worthily all my days so that when I go hence I may leave behind me a record of work well done".
**Honor Edwards
(Student 1923 - 25, Staff 1925 - 31)**

ILLUSTRATION OVERLEAF; 'Holidays' by Mary Peet, who was a student of the Rachel McMillan Training College from 1929 to 1932. Her drawings, paintings and designs have been kindly donated to the McMillan Legacy Group.

THE McMILLAN LEGACY 1931 - 78
by Hayley Trueman

The death of Margaret McMillan did not hold back the fortunes of the Nursery School and the newly-opened Rachel McMillan Training College. Margaret McMillan's close friend and colleague Emma Stevinson now took up the responsibility for the running of the college, becoming its first Principal and Miss Campbell became the new head of the Nursery School.

When the college had opened in 1930 there were 75 students following a three-year McMillan and Froebel programme of study, with many others awaiting entry. Applications from prospective students came not only from Great Britain but also America, Canada, Germany, Russia, Sweden, Poland, Egypt and Malta. The first prospectus highlighted the College's continuing commitment to Margaret McMillan's philosophies: "We hope to turn out teachers who will be true gardeners of real child-gardens. And if these gardens are in the slum or mean area, so much the better, for they will make the slum a beautiful place in time, and make Edens out of mean streets."

The College, which had originally planned to take only ninety students, proved so popular that two further extensions had to be built in 1931 and again in 1937, to accommodate the growing numbers of students.

By the start of the Second World War, 140 students were studying at the training college. The Nursery had 270 children on its register and the Camp School had 80. In 1939 the College, the Nursery and the Camp School children all had to be evacuated out of the area, and out of danger from the increasing number of air raids on London. The College was evacuated to Hildenborough, Kent, and the Nursery and Camp School children to Kensing, Wrotham and Ardingly. Sadly, the evacuation also marked the permanent closure of the Camp School.

Evacuation meant extra duties and

Emma Stevinson, First Principal of the Training College

Our watchword is a simple one. It is also a very humble and yet aspiring utterance "learn to succour the helpless". We shall succeed and prevail in the measure in which we keep true to its spirit and aim. We must learn as no generation before ever learned, to succour the young children of all classes; but above all to help and uplift the poorest, the most neglected and the most helpless.

**Margaret McMillan,
Letter to Students, 1928**

responsibilities for some staff. Mary Clarke a young teacher at the Nursery, was sent away with 76, two, three and four year olds to Ardingly. With only the support initially of one other teacher, four assistants and a cook, she had to care for small, frightened and homesick children. Mary Clarke stayed with the children at Ardingly for the duration of the war. No doubt the experience proved to be valuable as she later went on to become the head of the Clyde Street Nursery School and eventually of the Rachel McMillan Nursery School in 1949, where she stayed until 1974.

During the 1940s major changes were taking place in education. The pre-war Haddow Report and the 1944 Education Act had brought about massive restructuring of the school system. Liberal child-centred approaches to education were being actively encouraged, and formal didatic teaching methods were being questioned. The Rachel McMillan Training College with its McMillan and Froebel trad-

ition welcomed the changes, broadening its training programme to cover the whole of the primary age range.

Even in the face of major educational changes, the Nursery and College had always been and would continue to be interdependent. This singleness of purpose produced what could be described as an 'eco-system' of learning, with both establishments providing jointly, not only a centre for child and adult learning, but a community-focused care service. This was very much in keeping with McMillan's ideas, that young children need nurture, that the Nursery and College should develop close home and local community links, and that the children should have appropriately trained and well-qualified teachers and carers, who had received hands-on, as well as academic training.

By the 1950s the governors of Rachel McMillan Training College decided to ask the LCC to take over the running of the college: they recognised that there was neither the room nor the resources to allow the expansion and development needed in the face of the ever-increasing changes to education. Many other changes were underway at this time, including the gradual phasing out of the student uniform with their distinctive blue head scarves and the children's nursery overalls and hair ribbons.

In 1961 the LCC finally agreed to take on the responsibility of the College. The move away from being a private college was welcomed, particularly by its new Principal Mary Phuddephat (1962 - 78) who believed that, "it was essential that the LCC came in to rescue [the College], essential that it opened up to all kinds of people".

The next six years saw the college virtually rebuilt and substantially extended. Student numbers had risen to 420 by 1967. The new demands of the London University curriculum meant a more academic programme. New staff were appointed and new courses introduced. The library trebled in size and a full-time librarian was employed. Mary Phuddephat remembers "it was an exciting time."

In 1964 the College acquired a new annex at New Kent Road, giving more space for students during the restructuring work at the college building in Deptford. It also enabled the College in 1967 to start a four-year part-time teacher training course for mature students, the first of its kind in London.

The McMillan philosophy of child-centred experimental learning was endorsed by the Plowden Report in 1968. This report resulted in the extension of the early years approach to the whole of the primary age range. Mary Phuddephat was keen that students should receive a theoretical underpinning to this approach. They should come to understand that "what the child was experiencing was not incidental".

By the 1970s the College was offering training courses at certificate and BEd levels, a primary PGCE for

My first impression of Deptford was it was the most awful place I had seen but then the Art lecturer sent us out with a sketch book to the end of Deptford High Street and to where the bridge crosses the Ravensbourne. Instructions were that we were to look at the beautiful colours that were around us, especially in the tonal variations of the brickwork in the buildings. I looked around and was amazed. It altered my whole way of thinking and from then on I realised beauty could be seen anywhere as long as one looked for it.
Lily Dawson (Student 1959 - 62)

Many of us came from Conservative homes but experiences in Deptford led us into more radical politics.

The importance and value of pre-school education through play was drummed into us. Our training sent us out as missionaries and we're still trying to be missionaries in a non-receptive environment where misguided attempts are being made to enforce inappropriate central control on what it is thought pre-school children should be achieving. Our training put the needs of children as individuals first and did not seek to impose goals unless and until they were ready to achieve them.
Susan Mills (Student 1959 - 62)

Some of the staff were quirky but that was part of the experience and stimulation. The practical side of training emphasised the ideal of 'trying for oneself'. This made one realise how individual children could be helped but didn't help one organise activities and keep control of a whole class.
Rosemary Allday (Student 1959 - 62)

postgraduate students and in-service training for teachers. In spite of the efforts of the Rachel McMillan Training College, it was to fall victim to the Government's reorganisation of teacher training which led to the closure of many colleges in London. In 1977 the College was amalgamated with Goldsmiths College, and the Annex with Southbank Polytechnic. Since then the college has passed from Goldsmiths into the hands of the University of Greenwich. Sadly, the College has stood empty since 1997 and its future is presently unknown.

The Nursery itself is still thriving, in spite of the loss of the College. Its principles are still firmly rooted in the McMillan tradition of learning through play, which it has successfully adapted to meet the needs of a multi-cultural Deptford. Most importantly it is managing to hold onto its essence, its ideas, in the face of Government policies that are increasingly moving early years education away from the use of child-centred, play-based learning. Margaret McMillan, no doubt would be outraged with the present state of affairs. And if she were with us today undoubtedly she would be making a nuisance of herself on the steps of the Department of Education.

THE LEGACY SURVIVES
by Emily Adlington

Rachel McMillan Nursery School is still thriving today. Although Deptford remains one of the poorest areas in the country, there are certainly not the same levels of disease, dirt, and infant mortality. So the emphasis on strict hygiene and health is no longer the primary focus of the Nursery School.

To explore the way Margaret McMillan's ethos operates today we can look at the school in terms of the four areas discussed above:
• Nurture
• Appropriate Education
• Parental Involvement
• Staff Training

Nurture remains the foundation for learning, although the physical side is no longer a necessary part of the school day, thanks to an overall increase in health and hygiene and the fact that families have the facilities to keep their children clean and no

longer have to live without a bathroom. Children arrive at school between 9 and 9.30 am and leave between 2.20 and 3 pm. Parents, carers and younger siblings are welcome to stay in the school during these times and to be a part of whatever may be happening. The principle of caring for the all-round development of the child remains very evident in the atmosphere of the school which values each individual child. The curriculum appears to work at providing a holistic approach.

In terms of the appropriateness of education, a continuation of Margaret McMillan's ideas is again apparent. The garden remains a primary focus and much of the work inside the shelters relates to nature as well as being part of an overall curriculum. The curriculum is imaginative; children are free to explore whilst being encouraged to learn new things by the staff. Staff are involved with groups of children, directing activities rather than running them.

An imaginative curriculum, apparatus and serious play

Observing nature helps in learning about colour, shape, pattern, number, classification and much more

Although Rachel McMillan Nursery School has 170 places it has a very spacious feel, both inside and out. Children are free to play outside or in and the shelters all have a veranda which enables outdoor play sheltered from the rain. Playing outside does not mean that a child will miss out on activities that may usually be done inside. Outside there are just as many activities as inside: painting, building, threading, reading and so on. Each shelter is planned to make sure all areas of the curriculum are met and children who may take to one particular sort of activity are encouraged to take interest in the others. For example, all children are encouraged to learn to write their name in the graphics area, which is often set out like some sort of office (eg, a post office). This captures the imagination and encourages children to 'play' at reading and writing.

Links between outside and inside can also be seen on the walls and in the art work. On one occasion a group of children had been observing and talking about snails after finding some in the garden. As a result of this a display was made of their drawings. Observing nature and using natural materials in play or art not only provides a feast for the senses but helps in learning about colour, shape, pattern, number, classification and much more. Such activities also encourage discussion which furthers language development. This is just one example of how staff at the nursery will use something that has captured children's excitement and imagination and turn it into a wealth of learning experiences.

There is a diverse ethnic mix in the nursery and approximately 40 different languages are represented amongst the families here. Margaret McMillan's fight against the prejudices of her day is echoed in the importance of equal opportunities within the nursery today. Around the buildings posters, books, dolls and messages written in numerous languages serve to promote an atmosphere that values and reflects each individual within the community.

Parents are sill a vital part of the nursery. When a child begins nursery there is a four-week settling in period and this may be extended if it is felt that a child needs it. This seems very long compared to most nursery schools but the staff here feel it enables both child and parents to feel happy and comfortable and is also very helpful for forming strong staff/parent relationships. Parents appear to be very supportive and parents' meetings usually have 100% attendance. There is a parents' room and three times a week there is a toddler group in the nursery which is run by the parents.

Specialised training was a core part of Margaret McMillan's approach and, like everything in her work, she designed it herself. Now that Rachel McMillan is a state nursery and training is no longer offered in the college next door, staff at the school hold the usual qualifications needed to work in any state nursery. In terms of learning and studying the ethos of Margaret McMillan, the Headteacher is definitely a 'McMillanist' and has an extensive knowledge of how a school can be run on Margaret's principles. Therefore, the passing on of her ideas to staff today is very important. INSET days are spent learning, discussing and reinforcing a modern version of the McMillan approach and curriculum planning is still very much based on her theories. Although there is no longer specialised training for staff at the school, staff appear to be actively supportive and aware of McMillan's philosophy.

Curriculum planning still sees each child as an organic entity and seeks to cater for the fact that all aspects of child development are inter-related. There is positive teamwork in the classrooms and students are very much a part of this. On my visits to the school staff were well spread around the activities, involved with the children, directing when necessary but

Taking a breather on a sunny day in the garden

The Hoggan triplets – a Deptford family at the Nursery

not ruling. Language is an important part of each activity and staff seemed to be taking a leading role in directing discussions and introducing new words.

The focus on the importance of the local community has continued since Margaret McMillan's day. Family involvement remains crucial and parents often come in to share or run activities with the children. Local people such as policemen, shopkeepers, vicars and so on, come in to talk about the community as well.

Children are taken out on local visits. The Deptford High Street market, which runs three days a week, is often used as an opportunity to learn about the community, whilst also learning about colour, number, shapes, texture and so on. The focus on the community fosters a warm and open atmosphere in the school. The children are used to meeting lots of different people and, as a result, appear naturally inquisitive and polite towards visitors.

The community within the school itself is also very important. Everyone is viewed as learning together and everyone is encouraged to help each other. I encountered a good example of this when observing a group of children putting on their coats so that they could play outside. A number of children claimed they could not fasten their coats and requested assistance. Rather than obliging, the nearby staff member began not only encouraging the children to try but also encouraged those who had done their coats up by themselves to help teach the others. Hence, this usually rather mundane task was turned into an exercise in community learning. It is the little situations such as these that count and can help to encourage a love for learning together. Margaret McMillan was constantly challenging presumptions and attitudes that she felt devalued children.

Facing the Challenges

The greatest recent challenge for Rachel McMillan Nursery School was a failed OFSTED inspection in June 1997. This came as a huge shock to staff, parents, Greenwich Council's Early Years department and many people in the local community. Many feel that this failure devalued and misunderstood the work of the nursery. Parents remained supportive throughout and the governors wrote an article to the Education Secretary challenging the decision of the OFSTED report.

Since Rachel McMillan Nursery School went into 'special measures' there have been a couple of monitoring inspections carried out by HMI to assess the progress and re-evaluate the school. In contrast to the damaging OFSTED inspection, these have been very positive about the standard of education at the nursery. Many of the comments made by HMI at the first monitoring inspection after the school became subject to special measures showed the nursery as far from failing.

The only area of the report on the nursery that was termed 'unsatisfactory' related to safety issues in the playground and some areas of the building. This is not in any way a reflection on the education being offered or the management of the school. Rather, this is what inevitably happens to old buildings and gardens when there is a lack of funding and resources being given to their upkeep.

Despite the general positive tone of recent HMI inspections it is important to examine why Rachel McMillan Nursery School received a failed OFSTED inspection in the first place. To those who know of the school and are aware of early years practice, the inspection reveals a tension between what the nursery see as appropriate and what the Government see as necessary. OFSTED's main criticisms of the school were: the standard of literacy, especially writing, was below standard; some shelters appeared to be below national standard in mathematics; the children have too much choice which

• In all the lessons seen, children were attaining in line with their ages and stages of development.

• In most classes there is a happy learning environment where children are learning through good, structured experiences.

• The children are happy and enthusiastic learners. The relationships between the adults and children are good and the children are developing the important skills of independent learning.

Extracts from the first monitoring inspection after the school became subject to special measures, February 1998

[Miss McMillan] was far ahead of any that I know in teaching reading. "Read with the child. Get the child used to looking at the words, then read with him." There was no mention of breaking up words into sounds. "Let the child read so the words flow." When teaching reading I always found that her method was the best and most natural.
Gwen Yorath (Student 1920 - 23)

Miss McMillan had a lovely clear voice, and was forever telling us not to chop off our words... if you can imagine all of us practising our vowels, a-a-a-a, e-e-e-e, i-i-i-i, o-o-o-o, u-u-u-u, at the tops of our voices! It was hilarious!
Rosie Cawte (Pupil 1914 - 26)

Miss McMillan taught us to respect books. In turn she would make us librarians of our own library.
Dorothy Adshead (Pupil 1916 - 26)

results in progress being dependent upon chance; and punctuality is poor as there are flexible times at the beginning and end of the day.

In terms of language and literacy, the report acknowledged in its introduction that 62% of pupils are from ethnic minority backgrounds and for 43% of pupils English is a second language, yet it failed to discuss the possible effects of this on the overall outcomes in literacy and how provision has to match needs. Rather it simply noted that in this area the school was "below the national standard". Furthermore, the report acknowledged that a high percentage of pupils have special educational needs. Here again there was no discussion as to the effect this might have on overall attainments in literacy. This argument can also be used in response to levels of attainment in mathematics. From this it appears that the conclusion drawn by OFSTED in this area was based on benchmarks that do not allow issues such as English as a second

language or the level of special educational needs to be taken into account. Neither did the report discuss the learning processes that are taking place to encourage literacy. Perhaps this is because inspectors naturally looked for obvious signs of children being able to read and write, rather than examining what was taking place below the surface to encourage beginnings in literacy. Margaret McMillan held literacy to be very important but strongly felt that formal methods in the early years and premature forms of learning could do more harm than good. Palmer recently argued in the TES that the formal approaches towards phonics encouraged by OFSTED are not only unrealistic but dangerous. Children need to have the opportunity to develop their language skills through interaction and communication before being taught how to take a word apart and how to write it.

The criticism that children have too much choice and therefore that progress is dependent on chance is difficult to substantiate. Whether progress happens or not is never fully dependent on chance. Children have the ability to choose activities and explore for themselves. Many studies show that environments in which children are encouraged to direct their learning and have freedom of choice as opposed to formal teaching methods result in adults who are generally more stable, more involved in the community and less likely to commit crime.

Although on the surface it may look like certain levels of attainment are not being met, early years specialists acknowledge that we cannot always be sure of the outcome of nursery education until years later.

The OFSTED report had to acknowledge that the nursery works excellently with parents and stated that the involvement of parents and carers makes a "valuable contribution" to the school. However, in its criticism of the flexible times to the beginning and end of the day the report failed to examine the importance of these times in terms of the vital links between home and school. It was somewhat contradictory, therefore, to disregard their contribution to the school day at these times. Attendance at the nursery is good and a survey of how parents felt about the school carried out by the inspection team indicates clearly that parents approve of the education their children are receiving. No explanation was given as to why an OFSTED report could over-ride parental satisfaction. This appears to suggest that parents are not able to make adequate judgements about educational provision, and does not fit with policies of parental choice and diversity.

The report was positive about the school's work on equal opportunities, the good team-work of the staff, and the fact that, on the whole, children are self confident with good behaviour and relationships.

The governors' response to the OFSTED report focused on the way in

Specialists acknowledge that we cannot always be sure of the outcome of nursery education until years later

'Shouldn't we take the fire engine, sarge!?'

which the inspection was conducted. Firstly, not one of the inspectors was an early years specialist and none claimed to have any experience working in the nursery sector. As a result the governors doubted whether the inspection 'findings' could be fully credible. In 1995 an inspection was carried out in the nursery by the Borough of Greenwich inspectorate. This was remarkably positive about the school and it is puzzling to imagine that standards can so rapidly deteriorate. The governors pointed out "the only rational explanation of this is that different sets of criteria have been used. While the Greenwich inspection was focused on issues related to the quality of the educational provision being offered by the school, the OFSTED inspection has adopted a political rather than an educational agenda, a criteria of evaluation inappropriate to nursery provision."

This can largely be viewed as a difference in priorities. On the one hand McMillanism holds that learning processes ought to be regarded as most important in early years whilst it appears that the 'desired outcomes' set by SCAA are paramount to OFSTED. Processes need vision, imagination, child-centredness, and valuing of the importance of every aspect of each individual. Targets and outcomes, whilst necessary in a secondary role, are not a framework for education, only an imperfect measure of it.

The need for nursery education to be process-orientated as opposed to target-led is a philosophy that is held by many early years specialists. Pat Gura argues that the National Curriculum represents a 'legalistic' value system within which curriculum is primarily knowledge-based and leads to formal methods of teaching. This is contrasted with a 'moral' system that allows for freedom and imagination in early childhood curriculum. The moral view acknowledges that because children are all different they will reach goals by different means. In order for this to take place, young children need to have the freedom to explore and find independence. The 'desirable outcomes' of the National Curriculum, and the pressure of OFSTED inspections can create a system in which children are controlled and disenfranchised; objects rather than subjects.

In order for a child to develop as a whole, nursery provision must allow freedom and rest on the sensitivity of staff to know when to direct. Pressures to reach desired national averages too early "put at risk the delicate balancing act which children perform between advancing and withdrawing". This view echoes McMillan's attack on the rigidity of the elementary school system at the turn of the century.

The Early Years Agenda for the New Millennium (EYANM) is a group of early years specialists who recently called on the Government to rethink its nursery system. It is interesting to note how many of their proposals echo Margaret McMillan's vision for nursery education. For example, they promote the need to see early years education as the foundation of all learning. Like McMillan, EYANM believe nursery education must consider processes within learning and remember that sometimes 'outcomes' are not so easily measured. Wendy Scott points out that many studies have helped to show that three to six year olds 'learn by doing' and that teaching must be linked with exploration. This follows McMillan's work in creating an appropriate environment which naturally stimulates 'doing' and keeps teacher intervention sensitive and responsive to the child's exploration.

Margaret McMillan was one of the first in this country to see the importance of training for nursery education and initiate this. EYANM want to see this specialism brought back into teacher training. Although nursery education is currently for three to five year olds, it is interesting to note that EYANM want the government to extend this up to the age of six. This caters for natural stages of child development and is closer to McMillan's insistence

Nursery provision must allow freedom and rest on the sensitivity of staff to know when to direct

For years we called her 'crank'. We rejoiced in her complete knowledge, in the beauty of the similes with which her speeches were decked. We revered her worship of utter truth. We admired her devotion and intrepidity. We said she had a shining bold look like Santa Barbara... We loved to think of her as protectress of the children. But we called her crank, and said she had one idea. Now many of us think she had the one idea that matters.
'The Portrait Gallery'
The Woman Worker, 5 June 1908

that early education ought to continue to the age of seven. Family and community involvement are also noted as vital to early education.

The child centres of Reggio Emilia in Italy have been praised by early years specialists for their model of family and community involvement. There is a similarity of vision between these and Margaret McMillan. Everyone is encouraged to see early education as the responsibility of the community and the curriculum is very much centred around relationships between children, staff, families and community. Placing value and responsibility for early education into the hands of everyone not only encourages social development but fosters a community of learning in which all can take part. As well as a similar vision of the importance of the community, Reggio Emilia and Rachel McMillan Nursery School both prioritise the learning environment. Although on the surface these environments may be a little different, the underlying

philosophy is that young children, placed in a stimulating and loving environment, will naturally explore and develop their potential. Loris Malaguzzi, one of the founders of Reggio Emilia, felt very strongly that adults all too easily impose education onto children without realising that children hold within them "enormous potential" and that learning is "in large part due to the children's own doing, as a consequence of their activities and our resources". This matches Margaret's philosophy of growth as inherent and simply requiring nurture and appropriate education.

A Malaguzzi poem speaks of the importance of understanding the 'languages' of children and allowing these to develop. Similarly, Margaret saw these 'languages' as inter-related, that imagination and science belong alongside one another in the 'child garden' and that learning needs hands, head and heart. If the visionary philosophy of centres like Reggio

Emilia can be a model for nursery education, so too can McMillanism.

Despite the encouraging vision of many early years specialists, until a philosophy of 'wholeness' is embraced in early education, schools that seek to meet individual needs and allow children to speak their own 'languages' may continue to be forced towards a target-led curriculum.

Nursery education in Britain needs to return to a vision that sees the needs and 'languages' of nursery children rather than focusing on increasing academic results and competition with international neighbours. The ethos of Margaret McMillan, shared by many today, may in the long term be a more effective path towards achieving these results. In *Education Through the Imagination* Margaret ends by quoting Proverbs 29:18: "Where there is no vision, the people perish".

The child has
a hundred languages
a hundred hands
a hundred thoughts
a hundred ways of thinking
of playing and speaking
A hundred, always a hundred
ways of listening
of marvelling, of loving
a hundred joys
for singing and understanding
a hundred worlds to discover
a hundred worlds to invent
a hundred worlds to dream

The child has
a hundred languages
(and a hundred, hundred,
hundred more)
but they steal ninety-nine.
The school and the culture
separate the head from the body.
They tell the child:
to think without hands
to do without head
to listen not to speak
to understand without joy

They tell the child:
that work and play
reality and fantasy
science and imagination
sky and earth
reason and dream
are things
that do not belong together.
And thus they tell the child that
the hundred is not there
The child says: No way.
The hundred is there.

LORIS MALAGUZZI, 1993.

Frances Marriott, current
Headteacher of Rachel McMillan
Nursery School

THE NURSERY SCHOOL TODAY
by Frances Marriott

The Building

I was appointed as headteacher of the nursery in 1993. The Inner London Education Authority had been abolished five years earlier and the school, now under the administration of the London Borough of Greenwich, was showing the first signs of neglect.

One of my first meetings with the Director of Education was about the possibility of annexing all six of the Greenwich nursery schools to their nearest primary school. I knew this meant closing Rachel McMillan: it would not have been feasible to add such a large number of pupils (the other nursery schools being either a quarter or a third in size) onto an existing school. So began what has sometimes been a battle with the Local Education Authority (LEA). Through careful campaigning and discussion we convinced the Council on that occasion not to go ahead, and the six nursery schools survived.

Over the past ten years neglect has set into a beautiful and unique school. It is a mystery that Greenwich does not nurture, maintain and promote it. The design, with its wide verandas, beautiful grounds and London-brick buildings, is exceptional. Steeped in history it continues to command both a national and international interest. It needs completely refurbishing with new heating, flooring, furniture and equipment in each shelter. The staff block, office block and community rooms should be refurbished and modernised. Parts of the playground should be redesigned and much of it needs resurfacing. The bathrooms adjacent to each class need complete refurbishing and modernising. This work would be a true investment for future generations of children.

In July 1997 Rachel McMillan failed its OFSTED inspection, due in part to the neglected site. The LEA was forced into action as there were many recommendations relating to Health and Safety legislation. Essential work was carried out which included newly-decorated classrooms, new climbing equipment in some areas, bark pits around standing climbing equipment, new kitchens and cooking stations in every classroom, new carpet for book areas and a new, fully-resourced library. Alongside this work a successful bid to the Creekside Renewal Programme meant that other improvements relating to the heritage of the school could be made. This work has improved the site and raised standards enough to satisfy OFSTED.

It is still true to say that Greenwich Council needs to recognise the asset of Rachel McMillan Nursery School and support the school as it deserves. The potential is great and it should invest now for the future generations of children the nursery school will serve.

Philosophy and Practice

In 1989, under my predecessor Marjorie Ouvrey, staff, governors and parents published a curriculum document. This emphasised the importance of learning through play in the formative years and explained the educational value of every activity used in the school. It mapped out activities and experiences to cover each area of the early years curriculum.

In 1994 I reviewed this document to include a holistic approach to teaching and learning. It was now more explicit for staff to consider the child at the centre, embraced by his or her family, heritage languages, gender and neighbourhood community.

Our practice considered a child-centred approach based on the knowledge and understanding of child development. We placed (and still do) great value on play and first-hand experiences and the rearing processes involved. We recognised the importance of spontaneous learning from the individual children's interest. We believed firmly that, during the formative years, rates of learning vary from child to child and that this diversity of developmental levels – intellectual,

A birthday party at the Nursery

Successive governments have tried different approaches to Early Years: milk-snatching to target-madness...

physical, social and emotional – must be catered for.

Much of our practice and philosophy is based on the early childhood educators – McMillan, Froebel, Isaacs – and reinforced by the most recent research of Hurst, Blenkin and Kelly, Lally, and Bruce. One of the reasons we failed the OFSTED inspection was a lack of understanding about how very young children best learn. The lead inspector relied heavily on a team member she thought was knowledgeable in early years education. Sadly, this was not the case. She wanted to see controlled small group work and, I suspect, sterile, safe environments. Great emphasis was placed on outcomes rather than processes. There is a current Government-led trend in this country to push younger and younger children into more formal approaches. Again the OFSTED team adhered to this school of thought. At Rachel McMillan we believe this is ill-informed, harmful and not in any young child's best interest. However,

to get out of special measures we needed to make changes that would satisfy OFSTED. I was concerned that our good practice would prevail and it was a great challenge to work out ways of satisfying OFSTED without compromising the McMillan philosophy. I think this was achieved. We came out of special measures within a year.

The People
Rachel McMillan is probably the largest nursery school in the country. It serves a school community of 170 full-time equivalent pupils and their families. Parents and carers are most important to us and we pride ourselves on a close partnership with them. It is a typical inner city multiculturally diverse school and embraces over 20 different heritage languages. Alongside English, Yoruba is the majority heritage language. We have a full-time Yoruba-speaking classroom assistant who not only supports the pupils but keeps the staff well informed of the Yoruba culture and helps bridge the

[72]

gap between home and school.

Many of the children attend for four terms before going on to primary school. Unfortunately, the Lewisham admission policy with its two points of entry has meant that for the last two years some children have been leaving to go into reception classes after only three terms and before they are ready. This affects more and more of our children as 80% of the intake live in the borough of Lewisham.

There is a large staff of 30. These include teachers, nursery nurses, class assistants, administration officers, kitchen and cleaning staff and a premises manager. We invariably have students training alongside us and are in partnership with Goldsmiths College, University of Greenwich and Lewisham College in the training of nursery teachers and nursery nurses.

The school welcomes visitors from all over the world. We regularly host parties of early years educators from America, Scandinavia, India and Japan. These visitors are interested in the history and philosophy of the school. Some of the links can be traced back to teachers who came from abroad to train at the Rachel McMillan Training College. Often these teachers, many of them retired, revisit. Ex-pupils return again and again to reminisce with vivid stories of their time at Rachel McMillan. Their memories of teachers, classrooms, gardens, rocking horses, and so on, never cease to amaze me. It seems that Rachel McMillan holds an important place in many, many memories.

The Future

In 1997 I joined the McMillan Legacy Group, along with the Chair of Governors, Jayne Day. One of the group's aims was to reclaim the empty Training College building, vacated by the University of Greenwich, and open it as a children and family centre. While this remains uncertain, the school lives on and could easily meet some of the innovative plans set out by the Legacy Group.

Visitors from Botswana, 1973

The children can't wait...

I intend to continue the debate with Greenwich LEA and would like to see the Nursery School converted to a children's centre offering both care and education, with facilities for under-twos, and three to five year olds. These facilities would offer a range of services including an extended day programme, a toy library, a community project worker, a speech therapist on site, and perhaps a holiday scheme for older children.

To meet the needs of our many visitors involved in research we need to house the McMillan archives which are currently inaccessible, and to open a small museum to the history of the open-air school movement and the lives and work of the McMillan sisters.

The Rachel McMillan Nursery School is an important and significant school. It is part of our local and national heritage. Recognised as such it could evolve into a leading institution of the 21st century, continuing the vision of Margaret McMillan almost a century ago.

RESCUING THE LEGACY
by the Deptford Discovery Team

The McMillans have re-entered our lives over the past few years. Everywhere we turn there's another piece of the legacy that needs rescuing: sometimes a physical building, sometimes a point in a policy debate.

Alongside the McMillan Legacy Group, the Deptford Discovery Team (DDT) has been developing and restoring the Rachel McMillan Nursery grounds and has created the McMillan Herb Garden on derelict land next to Heather's Vegetarian Restaurant. In line with McMillan's emphasis on the child-garden, the new Herb Garden, funded by Groundwork's *Vital Centres & Green Links* SRB programme, offers children at the Nursery and other local schools opportunities to learn about 'living and growing' and the food element of Design & Technology. In addition to its curriculum value, the walled garden is used by the local after-school club and opened regularly to the public.

Across the street, DDT have also overseen the restoration of the St Nicholas' churchyard and the creation of a Local Studies resource in the old Sunday School rooms.

The McMillan 'ownership' of the Deptford Green site has been consolidated by these developments, which together create a 'vital centre' in the most historic part of Deptford.

In the Nursery itself, the Groundwork in Education programme has assisted the school in addressing health & safety concerns while creating a whole-school plan for the playground areas. A number of problem areas identified by the OFSTED report were treated as urgent and funded through Greenwich LEA. Although this was not the ideal way to begin a grounds development project, which requires whole-school participation in planning, DDT helped ensure that the emergency works were part of an imaginative and flexible design and incorporated the new features into a more holistic approach to the grounds.

The Deptford Green area is now the site of environmental improvements, including the McMillan Herb Garden (on the derelict corner site to the west of the nursery)

The children love the herbs. The toddlers press the leaves with their tiny fingers, and come into the shelter smelling their hands.
Margaret McMillan, The Nursery School, 1919

Music workshop at the Nursery
with Cor Blimey! Arts, 1999

The Environmental Development Group, which represents each shelter, parents, governors and premises staff, was started by teacher Liz Buck in spring 1999 and grounds development became a focus for educational activities over the summer term.

An underspend in the Creekside Renewal SRB programme led the Nursery to bid for funds for other priority improvements. The bid was successful and facilitated another phase of restoration and development projects, again overseen by DDT. These included reclaiming the roof garden above Shelter Three, renovating the Margaret McMillan memorial lamp, rebuilding the 1930s Hovis bread-cart, reinstating the parents' seat around the London Plane tree and establishing raised herb beds near the entrance to the school.

Entrance works, including resurfacing, a 'musical' barrier, wall reliefs and new signage, were designed and installed with guidance from school staff, inspiration from the Mary Peet archive, and reference to the school's rich history.

This phase included the development of a music garden through a day of music workshops run by local artists, and consultation over a level change which isolates one classroom from the rest of the school. The level change issue engaged the whole school in finding a creative educational solution to a technical access problem. Their ideas and drawings were brought together by Jon Cook into a 'Water Cycle Steps' proposal *[see p. 82]*.

The McMillan Legacy Group's proposals for the Training College building and their potential impact on the school site have encouraged a holistic approach to the development of the 'McMillan Island' site as part of the vital centre at Deptford Green.

THE McMILLAN LEGACY GROUP

Objectives

· to investigate and raise awareness of the unique approach of the McMillan sisters and its relevance today
· to support and develop future uses for the legacy instiutions which serve the children and families of the Creekside area
· to promote greater understanding of the needs of children in contemporary society and develop initiatives to meet these needs

The McMillan Centre for Children & Families

The McMillan sisters created an 'eco-system' of what we would now call 'early years services', including the clinics, camps, nursery school and training college in Deptford and the holiday centre at Wrotham, Kent. The key legacy institutions (those which survive) are the Rachel McMillan Nursery which continues to thrive, the Field Studies Centre at Wrotham and, most urgently, the Training College building on Creek Road which has been empty since August 1997 with no firm plans for re-use.

Over the past 18 months, the Legacy Group has been developing proposals for a Centre for Children & Families which would recreate the early years eco-system to honour the McMillan legacy by serving the needs of children today and tomorrow. We are hoping to work in partnership with Goldsmiths College to achieve a permanent legacy to the revolutionary work of the McMillan sisters.

The McMillan Centre proposal is for a holistic community-based resource bringing together a range of health, education and welfare services for children and families. Rather than duplicating existing or planned local provision, the Centre will complement and publicise them. It will be a focus for services and a network for people who are too often isolated.

The Centre will commemorate the work of Margaret & Rachel McMillan in Deptford and Greenwich and make their legacy relevant to today's local children and families. The Nursery and the new Centre will collaborate to provide quality services, particularly around training opportunities and out-of-school activities.

Ideas for services and activities in the Centre have been gathered at local public meetings and through a series of workshops with professionals in the fields of childcare, health and education. They include the following:

Out of School Services
After-school clubs
Training in after-school care
Summer play schemes
Arts & sports activities

Health Services
Community health clinics
Health promotion
Homeopathy, alternative therapies

Parenting/Nurture
Parenting skills training projects

Support for one-parent families
Babysitting network
Parenting advice & education

Information
Referrals/signposting service
Places to go/things to do with kids
(after-school clubs, playgrounds, childminders, crèches, nurseries)

Educational Services
Educational toys & equipment
Children's books
Toy fairs & manufacturers' trials
Toy-making/games workshops

Early Years Training
Early years units in teacher training
Seminars & conferences
Childcare resource room
Childminders' training/support

Research/Archive
McMillan archive & photo collection
Academic child-related research
Museum of childcare (international & historical)

Community Resource
Meeting rooms
Start-up space for new groups
Flexible hire terms
Community outreach

The McMillan Legacy Group has undertaken detailed research into the history and ethos of the McMillans. This has included tracking down and listing the scattered archive and photographic collections relating to the sisters, as well as gathering reminiscences from former staff, students and pupils.

Please show your support by joining the McMillan Legacy Group, c/o 441 New Cross Road, London SE14 6TA. Membership is free but donations will help us to continue our work.

Designs and costings for a
nursery school by
Mary Peet, c. 1929

ILLUSTRATION OVERLEAF (P.82):
'Water Cycle Steps' proposal by
Jon Cook of Deptford Discovery
Team for dealing with the level
change at Rachel McMillan Nursery School. Based on ideas from
children and staff, 1999.

Cost of the building and furnishing of the Nursery School...........

	£	s	d
Cost of the school without land	4,000		
Cost of one shelter	750		
Furnishing of one shelter ...			
40 chairs @ 3/4	6	13	4
10 tables @ 12/6	6	5	
40 seater beds @ 8/-	16		
40 blankets @ 8/9 [red]	17	10	
45 mugs @ 6d [enamel]	1	2	6
40 plates @ 5d "		16	8
40 spoons small @ 3d		10	
10 spoons large @ 4d		3	4
5 dishes @ 8d		3	4
3 ladles @ 1/-		3	
40 towels ½ yd each @ 1/- yd	1		
40 flannels ¼ yd each " " "		10	
40 tooth brushes @ 4½d		15	
40 hair brushes @ 9d	1	10	
40 combs @ 6d	1		
10 table cloths 36×36 ins material 1/11 yd		19	2

Cost of furnishing continued

	£	s	d
4 wastepaper baskets @ 2/11		11	8
6 flower vases @ 1/6		9	
Piano [secondhand]	10		
Large chair		4	11
First Aid Box		7	6
Sundries			
3 jugs @ 1/-		3	
1 knife @ 6d			6d
4 nail brushes @ 6d		2	
3 fire guards @ 15/-	2	5	
Pegs for bathroom & cloakroom @ 3d	1		
Total cost for furnishing the shelter	69	14	11

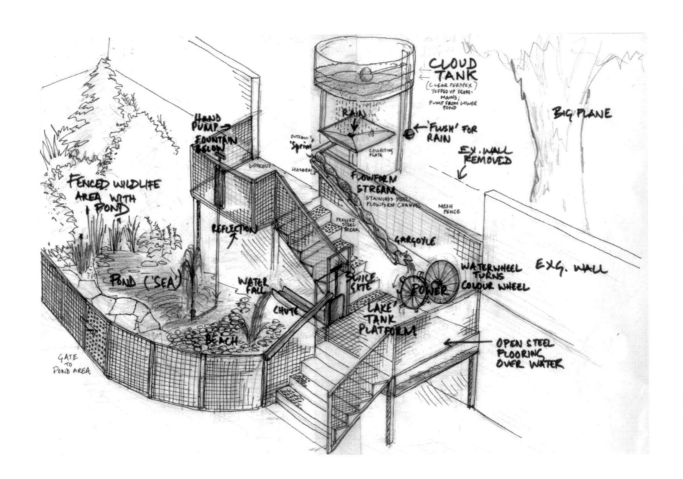

CLOUD
TANK
(CLEAR PERSPEX)
TOPPED UP FROM:
MAINS;
PUMP FROM LOWER
POND

RAIN

← 'FLUSH' FOR
RAIN

BIG PLANE

COLLECTING PLATE

OUTLETS
'SPRING'

HANDRAIL

E.X. WALL
REMOVED

FLOWFORM
STREAM
STAINLESS STEEL
FLOWFORM CHANNEL

MESH
FENCE

HAND
PUMP

FOUNTAIN
BELOW

LOOKOUT

FENCED WILDLIFE
AREA WITH
POND

REFLECTION

GARGOYLE

WATERWHEEL
TURNS
COLOUR WHEEL

E.X.G. WALL

POND ('SEA')

WATER
FALL

SLUICE
GATE

POWER

CHUTE

LAKE/
TANK
PLATFORM

PRESSED STEEL
STREAM

BEACH

GATE
TO
POND AREA

OPEN STEEL
FLOORING
OVER WATER

SOURCES

Ballard, P B
Margaret McMillan: An Appreciation

Bradburn, E *Margaret McMillan: Framework & Expansion of Nursery Education* (1979)

Bradburn, E
Margaret McMillan: Portrait of a Pioneer (1989)

Gura, P 'An Entitlement Curriculum for Early Childhood' in *Education in Early Childhood: First Things First* (1996)

Gura, P (ed) *Reflections on Early Education & Care: Inspired by Visits to Reggio Emilia* (1997)

HMI Monitoring Report, Rachel McMillan Nursery School (Feb 1998)

Kent, J & P *Nursery Schools for All* (1970)

Kimber, J *Famous Women of Lewisham* (1986)

Leach, W 'In Memory of Margaret McMillan', *The Labour Woman* (May 1931)

Lord, M 'Margaret McMillan in Bradford': Fourth Margaret McMillan Lecture (1957)

Mouatt, K 'Time for Reflection', *Nursery World* (5 June 1997)

Oftsed *Summary of Inspection Report* (1997)

Palmer, S 'Too Much Too Soon', *Times Educational Supplement* (17 Oct 1997)

Parkin, J 'From the Bottom Up, *Times Educational Supplement* (10 Oct 1997)

Rachel McMillan Nursery School Inspection Report: Response of the Governing Body (1997)

South Eastern Herald 'The Opening of the Deptford Clinic' (22 July 1910)

Steedman, C *Childhood, Culture and Class in Britain: Margaret McMillan, 1860-1931* (1990)

Steele, Jess *Turning the Tide: The History of Everyday Deptford* (1993)

Steele, Jess *The Streets of London: The Booth Notebooks* (1997)

Steele, Jess (ed) *Deptford Creek: Surviving Regeneration* (1999)

Sylva, K 'The Early Years Curriculum: Evidence Based Proposals' (unpublished paper, presented to SCAA in Summer 1997)

The Woman Worker
'The Portrait Gallery' (5 June 1908)

Pupils, students & staff quoted in the text
Dorothy Adshead (Pupil 1916-26)
Rosemary Allday (Student 1959-62)
Winifred Bonny (Student 1925-28)
Winifred Brown (Student 1928-31)
Alice Campbell (Head of Baby Camp and Nursery School 1925-45)
Lily Dawson (Student 1959-62)
Honor Edwards, (Student 1923-25, Staff 1925-31)
Gladys Harvey (Student 1918)
F. Hawtry (Principal, Avery Hill Training College, 1922)
Margaret Lamming (Student 1923 - 25)
Dorothy Lob (Pupil 1920-28)
Lily Lynn (Pupil 1929-38)
Dr Albert Mansbridge, Speech at Commemoration Service, 1950
Susan Mills (Student 1959-62)
Mary Peet (Student 1929-32)
Peggy Shade (Pupil 1925 - 32)
Emma Stevinson, Rachel McMillan Training College Newsletter, July 1931
Gladys Woodhams (Pupil, 1920s)
Gwen Yorath (Student 1920-23

ARTICLES BY MARGARET McMILLAN

The Bradford Labour Echo

'The Ventilation of Schools' (15/5/1897);
'School Board Notes' (18/9 & 25/9 & 22/10/
1897); 'Physical Training' (12/11/1898); 'Art
Training in Board Infant Schools' (19/11/
1898); 'Rest' (21/1/1899); 'An English Kindergarten (25/3/1899); 'Baths' (13/5/1899)

Child Life

'Child Study: Fatigue' (July 1904); 'The Child
Under Five: Suggestions...'(Jan 1905); 'True
and False Applications of Froebel's Prin-
ciples' (July 1905); 'Child Labour' (Oct
1908); 'Waiting' (Jan 1910); 'Dress in
Elementary Schools' (June 1910); 'Nursery
Schools of Tomorrow and their Effect on
Education in Schools' (1919)

Christian Commonwealth

'In a School of Today' (24/2/1909); 'Near the
Flame and the Shadow' (10/3/1909); 'Ten
Hundred Thousand Philips' (24/3/1909);
'Homes of England' (7/4/1909); 'All Around
the Problem' (12/4/1909); 'Diary of a
Dayschool Scholar' (5/5/1909); 'The Problem
of Child Life' (9/6/1909); 'Secrets of the
Child Soul' (7/7/1909); 'Lifeboat on the
Ocean of Suffering' (21/7/1909); 'Socialism
and Health' (18/8/1909); 'A Danish Festival'
(29/9/1909); 'The Great Awakening' (3/11/
1909); 'The Christmas Rose' (8/12/1909);
'Philip's Christmas Day' (8/12/1909); 'A Visit
to a Danish High School' (29/12/1909);
'Physical Education' (5/1/1910); 'The First
Medical Report from Whitehall' (19/1/1910);
'One of the New Army' (26/1/1910); 'Mary
Jane' (2/2/1910); 'The London County
Council Election: What We Should Demand'
(23/2/1910); 'About Some Who Have Taken
the Plunge' (9/3/1910); 'The Serf and his
Son' (13/5/1910); 'The Tooth Clinic and
Kindred Matters' (13/7/1910); 'A Flower in a
Slum' (14/9/1910); 'At Deptford Again'
(19/10/1910); 'Johnny and Me' (2/11/1910);
'Education in America: Miss Margaret
McMillan's Impressions' (18 Jan 1911); 'The
Child Coal Heaver' (15/3/1911); 'Means and
Ends in Education Today' (9/8/1911); 'Bob's
Christmas Day' (6/12/1911); 'Marigold: An
English Mignon' (3/1/1912); 'The Montessori
System' (26/6/1912); 'In An Indian School'
(14/12/1912); 'Backward Children: A New
Method of Teaching' (29/1/1913); 'The New
Programme in Education' (26/2/1913);
'Children of Deptford: Findings of the Fourth
Report of the Deptford Health Centre'
(29/10/1913); 'The Faith I Live By' (10/12/
1913); 'Interview With Miss Margaret
McMillan: The Schools of Tomorrow' (21/1/
1914); 'At the Foot of the Rainbow'
(10/2/1915); 'Romance of the Slums'
(7/4/1915); 'Baby Week' (4/7/1917); 'The
Labour Programme: In Our Garden'
(13/2/1918); 'The Fate of Lennie'
(16/10/1918)

Christian Socialist

'A Sign of the Times' (Oct 1889); 'The Church
and Socialism' (Dec 1889); 'Liberty' (April
1890); 'Labour: the Mother of Capital' (June
1890); 'Evolution and Revolution' (August
1890); 'Help' (April 1891)

The Clarion

'Drink in Labour Clubs' (24/2/1894); 'Music
in Labour Clubs' (3/3/1894); 'The Women of
the ILP' (16/3/1894); 'A Halt on the Hill'
(14/5/1894); 'Socialism in a Highland Kirk'
(21/5/1894); 'A Woman of the Age of Gold –
Mary Muse' (8/9/1894); 'To All Overworked
Mothers' (29/9/1894); 'To All Overworked
Men' (27/10/1894); 'Two Friends' (11/11/
1894); 'Silicon, Maid of Much Work' (16/3/
1895); 'The Two Conquerors' (6/4/1895);
'One of the Trespassers' (11/5/1895); 'Zoë'
(9/3/1895); 'Mistress and Maid' (1/6/1895);
'Mary's Lover' (15/2/1896); 'The Half Time
System' (12/9/1896); 'The Half Time System:
Part II' (19/9/1896); 'Voice Production in
Board Schools' (28/11/1896); 'The Education
of Children: A Half Hour in the Assembly

Room of a Board School' (14/11/1896); 'Growth' (20/2/1897); 'Lola' (27/2/1897); 'Lola: A Conclusion' (6/3/1897); 'A la Salpêtrière' (29/5/1897); 'The Subconscious: The Lorelei' (12/6/1897); 'Marie Bash Kirsteff's Grave' (26/6/1897); 'Levana' (14/8/1897); 'In The Pantheon' (11/11/1897); 'The Inn Keeper's Daughter' (18/12/1897); 'Children's Corner: Ann, A Tale for Children' (14, 21, 28/5/1898); 'Children's Corner: Tale of a Pearl Button' (7/1/1899); 'Tale of an Old Yew Tree: For Little People' (21/10/1899); 'The Clarion Round Table: A Reed Shaken in the Wind' (8/12/1900); 'Miss McMillan on the Fellowship' (5/1/1901); 'Schools and School Boards' (20/7/1901); 'Higher Grade Schools' (10/10/1901); 'The Stranger From Wonderland: A Fairy Tale' (7,14/3/1902); 'The Gifts That Cannot Be Stolen: A Child's Story' (11/7/1902); 'Dear Julia' (6/1/1905); 'What To Do Now' (25/4/1906); 'The Great Clause of the Education Bill' (8/6/1906); 'Germany and its Children' (22/6/1906); 'The School Doctor: How to Find Him' (13/7/1906); 'The Triumph for Childhood' (20/7/1906); 'Where Women Fight and Die' (17/8/1906); 'Women and the Franchise' (21/9/1906); 'Women in Prison' (2/11/1906); 'Why are the Germans Clean?' (17/6/1910); 'The Bradford School Clinic' (24/6/1910); 'An Instruction to the Clarion Fellowship: The Deptford Health Centre'

(29/7/1910); 'Deptford's Health Clinic: On Patients and Visitors' (4/11/1910); 'Camp Schools: The New Grant for the Children' (17/5/1912); 'To Save the Children: Work to be Done Now' (26/9/1913); 'Discipline' (24/10/1913); 'In the City of Sorrows' (28/11/1913); 'Religious Controversy and Education' (19/12/1913); 'The Power Stations of the World' (9/11/1914); 'The School Camp in December' (3/7/1914); 'Visions of the Heroes' (28/5/1914)

Co-operative News
'The Two Spectres' (22/9/1900); 'Schools and School Boards' (20/12/1900); 'A Great Social Problem: Feeding the Slum Children of Leeds' (1/10/1904); 'The Feeding of the Bairns: Jewish and English Children Compared' (6/11/1904); 'The Child at School: Speech Training' (7/1/1905); 'The Child's World: The Open School Commended' (14/1/1905); 'The School Clinic: What it is and What it is Not' (25/9 & 2/10/1909)

Ethical World
'Fatigue: Normal & Abnormal' (16/9/1899) 'A Forecast of Civilisation' (21, 28/10/1899); 'Literature and Children' (16/12/1899); 'The Literature of Children' (30/12/1899); 'The Loss of Mental Effort' (21/1/1900); 'Suppliant and Worshipper' (1/9/1900); 'The Government &

the People's Schools' (29/9/1900); 'Monasteries Old & New' (17/11/1900)

Ethics
'In the Islands of the Sea' (Feb 1903); 'A la Salpêtrière' (4/4/1903); 'Salvation Meeting' (11/4/1903); 'A Wesleyan Missionary Meeting' (25/4/1903); 'Topsy' (30/5/1903); 'The Office of a Teacher' (25/7/1903); 'Vivisection' (1/8/1903); 'The New Commission on Physical Culture' (8/8/1903); 'Infancy and Physique' (15/8/1903); 'Psychology of the Tramp' (22/8/1903); 'A School in the Western Isles' (5/9/1903); 'A Maid of the Isles' (19/9/1903); 'Ethical Teaching in a Yorkshire School' (26/9 & 10/10/1903); 'The Slums' (12/12/1903); 'An Old Chartist' (19/12/1903); 'Internationalism in Education' (13/12/1904); 'The Pottery School for Cripples' (20/2/1904); 'Ambidexterity in Schools' (9/4/1904); 'Ethics for Mothers' (23/4/1904)

Highway
'Worker and Student' (July 1909); 'Door of the North' (Sept 1909); 'A Day at Askov' (Oct 1909); 'New Ends and Purposes' (Nov 1909); 'Adolescence' (Dec 1909); 'The Claims of the Practical in Education' (Jan 1910); 'The First Medical Report From Whitehall' (Feb 1910); 'Vive la France' (Aug 1910); 'Notes on a

Closed Door' (Sept 1910); 'The Gardens Under the Sea' (Oct 1910); 'The People That Are Above Us' (Nov 1910); 'Higher Education and the Working Woman' (Dec 1910); 'The Second Medical Report From Whitehall' (Feb 1911); 'In the Middle West' (March 1911); 'Children of the Plain and the Forest' (April 1911); 'Joseph and Arnold Toynbee' (May 1911); 'In a Garden' (June 1911); 'With Arms Akimbo' (June 1911); 'In Our Garden - Chapterette II' (July 1911); 'Marigold – An English Mignon. (Kenst du das Land?)' (Sept 1911); 'In Holy Isle' (Oct 1911); 'Travellers Joy' (Feb 1912); 'In Our Garden' (May, June, July, Aug, Sept 1912); 'The New Education' (June 1913); 'Our Education System: The Education of Children Under Seven' (July 1913); 'Our Education System: Medical Treatment and What it Leads To' (Aug 1913); 'Jimmy' (June 1915)

The Labour Echo

'The Bacchanals' (11/5/1895); 'Demeter and Persephone' (25/5/1895); 'Ariadne' (1/6/1895); 'Pan' (8/6/1895); 'Hippolytus' (15/6/1895); 'The Beginning: According to the Greeks' (6/7/1895); 'A Living Wage' (9/7/1895); 'To the Electors' (11/7/1895)

The Labour Leader

'The Garden of Children: Froebel and the New Education' (Jan 1895); 'Tom Maguire: A Remembrance' (26/10/1895); 'A Woman of the Age of Gold – Mrs Heavytop' (8/8/1896); 'An English Kindergarten' (15/4/1899); 'Education in the Primary School' (27/5, 10, 24/6, 1, 8, 15, 22, 29/7 & 12/8/1899); 'Music Training' (12/8/1899); 'Four Ideals in Education I: The Military' (5/5/1900); 'II: The Aesthetic' (12/5/1900); 'III: The Monastic' (19/5/1900); 'IV: The Medical Ideal' (26/5 1900); 'Handel Stumm' (1, 15, 23, 29/9; 3, 10, 17, 24/11; 1, 8, 15, 23/12/1900; 19, 26/1; 2, 9, 16, 23/2; 2, 16, 23, 30/3/1901); 'Mending the Lives of the Little Ones: A Work Worth Peeping Into' (1/9/1905); 'The Higher Senses: Hearing' (4/4/1906); 'The Five Year Old at School' (6/4/1906); 'The Higher Senses: Seeing' (11/4/1906); 'The Education Bill' (18/4/1906); 'The Labour Party and the Children' (1/6/1906); 'In the Horse Yard' (15/6/1906); 'The Beginning of The End' (22/6/1906); 'Building Up The British Race' (6/7/1906); 'Shower Baths' (7/9/1906); 'Municipalisation of Hospitals' (28/9/1906); 'Free Meals' (22/3/1907); 'Penalties of Greatness' (26/4/1907); 'The Beginning That May Have to Halt' (17/5/1907); 'A Coming Conference' (26/7/1907); 'The Scholarship Child' (23/8/1907); 'After Echoes of the Congress on School Hygiene' (30/8/1907); 'The Star of Beauty' (18/10/1907); 'A New Epoch For Children' (22/11/1907); 'School Dinners Today' (29/11/1907); 'New Report of the Education Board' (1/1/1908); 'On The Embankment' (17/1/1908); 'Bradford Leads Again' (7/2/1908); 'From School to Embankment' (14/2/1908); 'A Special School Day' (28/2/1908); 'Apostles from Bradford' (17/5/1908); 'The New Act and how it works' (26/6/1908); 'Mr Leech's Reform' (10/7/1908); 'The Coming Conference' (31/7/1908); 'A British School Clinic and other matters' (25/9/1908); 'A London School Treatment Centre' (11/12/1908); 'The Care of School children: London Moves at Last' (15/12/1908); 'Schools and Hospitals' (8/1/1909); 'The School Clinic and Land Values' (15/1/1909); 'Land Raiders in Barra' (9/5/1909); 'School Clinics: Their First Fruit' (9/7/1909); 'Trades Union Congress & School Clinics' (3/9/1909); 'A New Kitchen' (12/11/1909); 'As the Echo Dies' (2/12/1909); 'The Children's Bread' (31/12/1909); 'Education and the Labour Conference' (4/2/1910); 'Medical Treatment in London' (17/6/1910); 'Faith and Fear' (27/1/1911); 'The Healers: April Night and May Morning' (25/5/1911); 'Save the Children: A Plea for the Social Treatment of Disease' (17/11/1911); 'How I became a Socialist' (11/7/1912); 'A Pioneer' (5/9/1912); 'The Child of the Future: when the stains are washed away' (26/12/1912)

The Labour Prophet

'Louise Michel' (Dec 1892, Jan 1893); 'Shop Life' (Jan 1893); 'Women of the Age of Gold:

Lady Fetherpoll' (Feb 1893); 'Silk Workers' (Sept 1893); 'Coal and Colliers' (Oct 1893); 'A True Capiltalist' (Dec 1893); 'My Experiences on the School Board' (Nov 1895)

The Two Worlds
'Three Leaves from a Deaf Man's Diary' (7/10/1898); 'Mona's Sister: A Christmas Tale for Little Folks' (10/12/1898); 'The Gifts That Cannot Be Stolen: An Allegory for Children of all Ages' (12, 19, 26/5 & 2/6/1899); 'The Silence of the Humble' (9, 16, 23, 30/6/1899)

Weekly Times & Echo
'Gutterella: A Woman of the Age of Gold (28/12/1895); 'Sorcha's Dream' (5/3/1905); 'The Robber: A Tale of the Hebrides' (6/9/1906); 'Ishbel's Return' (23/9/1906); 'The Alien' (26/3/1907); 'The Way of The River' (29/12/1907)

Woman Worker
'A Message of Spring' (May 1908); 'A Slum Mother' (3/7/1908); 'Clouds and the Rain' (17/7/1908); 'On Pleasant Speech' (11/9/1908); 'A Bard at the Braes' (25/9; 2, 9, 16, 23/10; 2, 9, 16, 30/12/1908); 'Medical Inspections of School Children' (6/1/1909); 'What Women are Thinking: The Child Slaves of England: Miss McMillan's Statement With Mrs Cobden Sanderson' (28/4/1909)

Young Socialist
'Toys' (March 1903); 'The School Mates' (Nov 1903); 'Neptune: A Dog' (Dec 1903); 'The Swifts' (March 1904); 'The Flower and the Rock' (June 1904); 'Arithmetic' (July, Aug, Sept 1904); 'A Fairy Tale by the Fairies' (Aug 1906, May, June, July, Sept, Oct, Nov, Dec 1907, Jan, Feb, March, April 1908); 'Jewels' (Feb 1907); 'The Hope of Spring' (March 1907); 'The Socialist Sunday Schools' (Feb 1908); 'A Story for Lilley' (July 1908); 'The Crow' (Aug 1908); 'The Little White Gull: A Story for Ishbel' (Feb 1909); 'The Garden Under Water' (March 1909); 'The Tree That Waited: A Story for Charlie' (April 1909); 'A Calendar of Socialist Saints: Biographies in Brief' (June 1909); 'Things That Talk' (July 1909); 'To a Little Friend Who is Ill' (Jan 1910); 'Clothes and How to Make Them' (July, Aug, Sept, Oct 1912)

Miscellaneous published articles
Child: 'The Deptford Health Clinic or Health Centre for Schoolchildren' (May 1911); *Christian World*: 'In Our Garden: An Experiment with Teddy' (27/3/1913); *Common Cause*: 'On Reports and Other Things' (25/4/1913); *Daily Herald*: 'In an Open Air Camp School' (3/1/1913); *Labour Women*: 'Laying the Foundations of Good Health: What Nursery Schools Can Achieve' (1/3/1928); *Morning*

Leader: 'The Fairway: Some East End Holiday Makers' (25/8/1910); 'The School Clinic: The Problems of Treatment Today' (24/11/1910); *New Era*: 'The Open-Air Nursery School' (1930); *School Hygiene*: 'On the Threshold' (Jan 1910); 'Speech Defects and Speech Training' (Aug 1910); *Scottish Health Magazine*: 'History and Aims of Open Air Nursery Schools' (April 1929); *Sheffield Guardian*: 'Nurseries for All Children' (March 1911); *Socialist Review*: 'Democracy and Higher Education' (1908); *Wheatsheaf*: 'Our Ailing Schoolchildren: And Then?' (Jan 1912); *Young Oxford*: 'Wanted, A Blend of Heroism and Specialism' (March 1901)

Essays, pamphlets and books

Samson, Clarion Newspaper Co, 1895
'Women in Relation to the Labour Movement'
in *The Labour Annual*, ed. J Edward, 1895
'The Women in the New Party' in
The New Party, ed. A Reid, 1895
Child Labour and the Half Time System, 1896
Early Childhood, 1900
'The Ethical End in Education' in *Ethical
Democracy: Essays in Social Dynamics*,
ed. Stanton Coit, 1900
'Child Labour' in *Dangerous Trades: Historical,
Social and Legal Aspects* (ed: T Oliver), 1902
The Beginnings of Education, 1903
The Mission of Children, 1903
Education Through the Imagination, 1904
*Economic Aspects of Child Labour and
Education*, 1905
Infant Mortality, 1906
*New Life in Our Schools: What it is and What it
is Not*, 1906
*The School Clinic Today: Health Centres and
What They Mean to the People*, 1906
Labour and Childhood, 1907
Schools of Tomorrow, 1908
'Women in the Past and the Future' in *The
Case For Women's Suffrage*, ed. B Villiers, 1908
The Child and the State, 1908, 1911
*London's Children: How to Feed Them and How
Not to Feed Them*, 1909
The Bard of Braes, 1909

A Children's Day, 1910
'Nurture Versus Education' in *The Needs of
Little Children, Report of a Conference on the
care of Babies and Children*, 1912
'The Case for the Industrial Woman' in *Men's
League on Women's Suffrage Handbook*, 1912
'The Camp School in *Transactions of the
National Liberal Club Political and Economic
Circle*, 1914
The Camp School, 1917
Nursery Schools and the Pre-School Child, 1918
The Nursery School, 1919
Hand-written draught of speech by Margaret
McMillan to the Froebel Society in Bradford,
1920 [document A2/13, Lewisham Local
Studies Centre]
What the Open-Air Nursery School Is, 1923
What the Nursery School is, Bradford
Froebel Society, 1926
The Life of Rachel McMillan, 1927